To my wife, Day,
who encouraged me in
this effort to help
Frederick Wilson
speak to our time

Lavinia Floyd greeting Henry Kate and Frederick after Retirement in Macon, Georgia at the home of Dr. Waldo Floyd

ACKNOWLEDGEMENTS

Thanks to:

- ❖ Dr. Martha Cain for pictures from the Statesboro period.
- ❖ Dr. Edwin Chase, South Georgia Conference Pastoral Counselor, for guidance in Publishing choices.
- ❖ Dr. Fred Craddock, Bishop C.W. Hancock, Dr. William H. Hinson and Bishop Richard Looney, for their quotes and encouragement.
- ❖ Lillian Davis of Macon, Georgia for designing the Front and Back Covers and giving other invaluable assistance.
- ❖ Mrs. John "Butch" Deaton of St. Paul United Methodist Church in Columbus for providing the picture of her grandson used at the close of "Transfiguration" and the quotes from the women in "Indelible Impressions".
- ❖ The Reverend C. G. Haugabook, Jr. for recording and Allene Haugabook for transcribing the sermon on Evangelism.
- ❖ The Reverend Don Kea for pictures from First United Methodist Church, Albany, and for the Resolution by the Deacons of First Baptist Church of Albany.
- ❖ Steve Rumford, Administrator of the Methodist Home for Children and Youth, for his encouragement and provision of some pictures.
- ❖ Victoria and Katherine, Frederick and Henry Kate's daughters, for pictures and countless hours of editing the manuscript.
- ❖ Contributors from Churches that had been served by Dr. J. Frederick Wilson who gave the funds for the cost of printing so that proceeds from all sales of the book could be given to The Methodist Home for Children and Youth of The South Georgia Conference of The United Methodist Church.

**Easter Sunday, April 10 1955, Frederick preaches to the 569 present at
First Methodist Church Statesboro, Georgia**

Contents

BIG WORDS FOR OUR TIME
by Dr. J. Frederick Wilson

The daughters of Frederick and Henry Kate at the Dedication of the J. Frederick Wilson Administrative Building at The Methodist Home for Children and Youth in Macon, Georgia

FOREWORD

J Frederick Wilson was born February 23, 1915 in Camilla, Georgia, the son of John Corbin and Nellie Whiting Wilson. Before his death on Christmas Eve in 1990, he had served in the South Georgia Conference of the United Methodist Church as Conference Youth Director; Pastor of the Jeffersonville Circuit; Teacher at Wesleyan College; U.S. Navy Chaplain in World War II; Teacher of Religion and Bible at Emory at Valdosta; Pastorates at Tennille; Statesboro First; Albany First; Vineville, Macon; and St. Paul, Columbus.

Donald M. Kea closed his Memoir in the 1991 Journal of the South Georgia Annual Conference by saying, "J. Frederick Wilson will be remembered as one of the giants of South Georgia Methodism. The one dominant, consistent theme in his preaching was the Love of God. All who ever knew him would agree that he lived that Love to the limit of human possibility. We miss him!"

As a fellow pastor who led singing in many of the Revivals he preached, and as the host pastor when I had him come to preach for me, I often begged Frederick to publish some of his sermons. He would always say. "Oh I don't have them written down anywhere, and, anyway, I have such an oral style that they wouldn't go over on the printed page. I'm so embarrassed when I see them written out after someone has recorded them—so many repetitions, so much language that seems impossible to punctuate."

I said, "But Frederick, you owe it to those coming after you, young preachers and others who could learn from your style and your warmth and your use of drama. They couldn't copy you exactly. No one would try to shoot a shotgun shell out of a BB Gun. But we could all learn from seeing how a master went about his handiwork."

I felt justified in this assessment when I shared some of his sermons with Dr. Fred B. Craddock, Bandy Professor of Preaching and New Testament, emeritus, at Candler School of Theology in Atlanta. Dr. Craddock wrote saying, *"While he preaches from Scripture, he does not hide in Scripture; he reveals much of his own good heart. His messages are made strong by: simple clarity; always good news; repetition which builds power; the use of conversation among characters in the sermon; personal appeal. I hope you preserve his oral style in your editing."*

When Dr. Wilson helped me in 1976 at First Methodist, Bainbridge, Georgia, I persuaded him to let me record some sermons and he asked for the copies that the secretary there had transcribed. But he never published. So recently I talked with his surviving daughters, Victoria and Katherine, who because of their Father's reservations reluctantly gave their permission for me to edit and publish a few of those sermons. They said, "We know how Daddy felt, but how can we say no to your wanting to do this?" I'm grateful to Victoria and Katherine for assisting me with some editing and for providing most of the pictures that you'll see in these pages.

This book is not just for all that knew and loved him. It is also for a new generation of seekers who delight in hearing a fresh Word from the Lord. It will enable hundreds who heard him preach to almost hear his voice again as they read these words and treasure anew the commitments they first made upon hearing him. It may also help a young preacher who never heard him to realize that his or her sermons don't have to be pedantic and sterile but can come to life in the voices and the personalities of the Bible.

Frederick and his beloved Henry Kate spent their retirement years in a home on the Campus of the Methodist Home for Children and Youth. He loved that institution and though he might still have some reluctance if he knew what I was doing, I think he might let me off since the proceeds of all sales of this little volume will benefit the Home.

The first nine sermons are nearly verbatim as Frederick delivered them. The last sermon in the book is one that I preached with heavy indebtedness to Frederick because I didn't have the tape, but only some notes that I had made when I heard him preach on RECONCILIATION. Two pages are devoted to some of his self-deprecating humor and two to some indelible impressions. At the end are four pages of faded but treasured photographs. Have a good read! It may be that as you read you may also worship the God who loves you. If that should happen, it may be the best reason for Frederick to forgive me.

W. Hamp Watson, Jr.

SHEPHERD
"The Lord is My Shepherd"
Psalms 23, John 10:1-18 KJV

Just one little idea to share with you on this our last Noontime meal together—we say almost by heart, many of us, the 23rd Psalm. And several times lately in my pastorate in funeral services, as an expression of our own faith as we stand there at the grave, I've asked everyone to join me in saying the 23rd Psalm. It's been very, very impressive because it is a great statement of faith—a tremendous statement of faith. It isn't sad, particularly. It certainly isn't in any way depressing. It's very uplifting. It's very hopeful. It's full of assurance and confidence. And it's so very beautiful as we all know. I've used it this way several times. I've asked the family. It's good therapy for them sitting at the side of the grave to hear themselves saying these wonderful words that are in the 23rd Psalm.

"The Lord is my shepherd." Jesus picked up on that idea, that beautiful symbolism of the shepherd and the sheep, and he said, as we very well know, *"I am the good Shepherd, and I know my sheep."*

And so we have from our Christ this same magnificent symbolism of a shepherd and a little lamb or sheep. And there is something about a sheep that we ought to understand—that Jesus had in mind, that certainly David had in mind when he began the

Psalm, *"The Lord is my shepherd,"* and when Jesus said, *"I am the good shepherd and know my sheep."*

I believe that there is no animal that is so dependent as a sheep—none—no four-legged animal any more dependent than a sheep. Can't run very fast so that if it finds itself being approached by an enemy it really is absolutely helpless. Hopeless for a sheep to run fast enough to escape a lion or certainly a bear or a wolf or any of the predatory animals that always like to find a flock of sheep somewhere. David, you will recall, told King Saul that this is how he got his training—with a sling, aiming it and firing it at the animals that would prey upon the sheep. This is why in that land the shepherd was so essential because the sheep sent out on the road or the range would be by themselves and at the mercy of the wild animals. They could never escape them.

All he had for protection was a little bleating voice. And actually, that was no comfort. And actually that was an enemy, too. If he were lost, particularly in the night, to use that little bleating voice would let the predatory animal know precisely where he was. The sheep is an animal that isn't very sure-footed. Walking along the rocky ground, walking near crevices or chasms, he's not sure-footed. And this is why the shepherd had his crook, and many a time he would reach out and take the sheep by its neck or take it by one of its legs and pull it back from a dangerous spot into which it had gotten. The sheep is a very dependent animal, has little strength of its own, little wisdom of its own, so easily lost because it has so little sense of direction, and no swiftness with which to escape the enemies that might approach it.

So David was acknowledging, *"The Lord is my shepherd."* I must be as helpless, as dependent in the living of my life as these sheep are in the execution of theirs. And just as they need a shepherd, so do I need a shepherd.

On the other hand, there is hardly an animal that gives more than a sheep does. There is hardly an animal that yields more for its master and its owner than a sheep does. I don't know how many times it gives its wool. And over and again it gives its wool, that warmest of all the fabrics that can also be so very beautiful and so soft. The sheep standing at the shearing gives generously of its wool.

It also gives of itself. It gives its meat. Maybe some people don't like lamb, the meat of the sheep. But in those countries where the sheep are, it's the salvation of those who own them because it is a source of meat. And of course today lamb is quite a delicacy. If you don't believe it, go see the price on it. And whether you acknowledge it by eating it—that it's a delicacy—you acknowledge it by the price that it demands. There's no animal that gives more in return for its keep than the sheep does.

And then in that olden day, it was the lamb that was most often taken to the temple and offered as a sacrifice for the sins of the family. So that the lamb, more often than any other animal, was used by the average Jewish family as its sin offering in the temple. I think Jesus must have carried a lamb with him on that twelve-year-old visit that he made to the temple in Jerusalem. Maybe it had been his responsibility to look after the lamb, to make sure that nothing happened to the lamb, to protect it so that there was no blemish on it, no damage ever done to it so that it would be acceptable as the sacrifice. The lamb gave its life as a sin offering for the family that brought it.

So at the same time that it is so dependent, it is also so important to the family that owns it. So dependent upon the shepherd, and yet so important to the shepherd. Jesus said, "I'm the shepherd. You are my sheep." And we see the picture so clearly in our own minds, don't we? We're so dependent, too—so much in this life that can hurt us, that can damage us, that can destroy us. So helpless, so easily lost, so unable to escape the ills of this life, so helpless and so dependent. And so he says, "I am the shepherd," and we lean upon the shepherd in our time of need.

And yet so important to the shepherd, you and I. He has no hands but our hands. He has no feet but our feet. He has no voices but our voices. He has no heart but our hearts to share with his children here on the earth where we live.

- If we don't use our hands,
  - if we don't use our feet,

- if we don't yield our hearts,
  - if our hands are not outstretched in compassion and love,
    - if our voices don't speak the good news of joy and peace and love,

then the shepherd is at a loss to have his work completed and his work done. So at the same time that we are so dependent **on** him, we are so important **to** him.

And you never get too old to be important to him. I said it Monday morning to those dear people out at the nursing home, we so often think that "doing" is the big thing. Everybody has got to be busy. Activity is the great thing. And we multiply this so in our minds that when we can no longer be busy and active, we can think that we are useless. But being is doing, also. I told them that some of the dearest people, some of the most important people, some of the most rewarding people that I know right now are people who can't be active. There are people who are handicapped, some old, some not old, but handicapped. But they're using the handicap in such a glorious fashion that what they **are** ministers. They don't need to be active to be important. They **are** something to us that ministers to us and serves us.

So let's gladly acknowledge our dependence on him and ask his help, but let's just as gladly and joyously render to him the service that he needs from us and feel, as he wants us to, how important we are to him.

Sometimes we can get pretty flippant about people who are getting old and sort of losing it. We tell stories like the one about the woman whose relative was checking on her in the nursing home to see how aware of reality she was. So she said to her, "Who am I?"

The woman said, "I don't know, but if you'll go up there to that desk and tell them your room number, they can probably tell you who you are."

But it can come home. It can get close to us. I remember being asked by the Chairman of the Pastor Parish Committee in one of my churches to call on his mother-in-law who had been a vital churchwoman but hadn't said anything relevant to him and his wife in weeks and she was approaching death. She just mumbled jargon of old popular songs and hymns mixed up together in an agitated way and didn't seem to know who they were when they visited her. I had the same experience with my visit, but as I sought to end it, I suggested that we recite the 23rd Psalm together. She didn't seem to even hear me, but as I began, "The Lord is my shepherd, I shall not want" she joined in and matched me word for word until we came to the words, "and I shall dwell in the house of the Lord forever." When I left the room, she was calm and full of peace. It wasn't but a few days before her shepherd came to lead her across the valley of the shadow of death to her final home.

Most of us are in our right minds here this morning, more or less. But I don't think it would hurt us to close this message by reciting as much as we can remember of this Psalm together. Would you join me in saying it? *"The Lord is my Shepherd"*.

PRAYER

We thank you, Father God, for both these facts—our dependence on you—our importance to you. Grant us the joy of acknowledging both in our daily lives—our need of you, and your need of us. Thank you for this happy time we've had together and give joy and peace to these your children. We pray in Christ's name. Amen.

EDITOR'S NOTE

J. Frederick Wilson was the consummate example of a Pastor who was himself a great shepherd not only to his own flock, but also to the entire community where he served. This is confirmed by excerpts from the resolution on the following page that was adopted by the Board of Deacons of the First Baptist Church of Albany when they learned that he was leaving First United Methodist Church, Albany.

A RESOLUTION

Adopted by the Board of Deacons of the First **Baptist** Church

Albany, Georgia

June 9,1964

"J. Frederick Wilson, who for the past nine years has served as Pastor of First Methodist Church... is recognized as the kind of preacher who comes our way once in a generation and the kind of pastor that every church desires and no church wants to lose."

"If ever there has been the slightest modicum of jealousy or envy between us, it was because at times we would discover a number of our very best members passing us by and going over to First Methodist to hear one of his heart-warming sermons. But to compensate for this, we are sure they always returned to us—if not better Baptists—finer Christians."

"With mixed emotions we bid him farewell, secure in the knowledge that wherever he goes, Frederick Wilson will always be found "feeding his sheep.'"

"And so, to our friend and brother in Christ, we wish to say, 'You have been a wonderful shepherd of your flock.'"

"And when the chief Shepherd shall appear, ye shall receive a crown of glory that fadeth not away." (I Peter 5:4 KJV)

INVITATION
"Behold, I Stand at the Door"
Revelation 3:20 KJV

I'm reading a verse that's very familiar to you out of the Book of the Revelation. I don't understand all of the Book of the Revelation, and I'm suspicious of anyone who says that they do. There are many passages I do not understand. And I'm counting on when I get there—and I **am** counting on getting there—that our Lord himself will have a Bible lesson. And we'll have a chance to go back into some of these wondrous pages and just have him talk about it. But there are some verses in the Book of the Revelation that I do understand. I understand all too well. And they are the ones that trouble me. Revelation 3:20 I understand, and sometimes it troubles me.

"Behold, I stand at the door and knock. If any man hear my voice and open the door, I will come in and sup with him and he with me." I haven't been all over this building, but I dare say that somewhere in the Sunday School rooms there may be one that has a painting that depicts this verse. It's a picture of our Lord standing at the door of a little cottage and he has a lantern in his hand. And the light reflects up into his wondrous face. Holman Hunt is the artist of that large canvas. And when it was done he was very, very grateful for it. He did not wish to sell it. And since he lived in the vicinity of London, he decided that he would give the painting to the City of London.

He requested that it be used where people could see it and maybe take a moment to stand in the presence of it and feel something of what was the message of the painting. He was distressed some months later when he went to London and visited a museum that he loved to visit and discovered that his painting was there. He was distressed that people had to pay to see it—having to pay to see our Lord standing at the door—the door of the human heart. And so he went home and took a canvas the exact size of the one he had painted before and repainted the picture of our Lord standing there. And he took it back to London when it was done, went to St. Paul's Cathedral, found the Chief Priest there in that magnificent cathedral and presented it to him. And it's there today. And if you're fortunate to go to London and are on your tour and are taken to St. Paul's Cathedral make sure that you see this painting.

If you're old enough to have stayed up late one night and watched the marriage of Prince Charles and Lady Di, or maybe saw it later on a re-run, then you saw the Cathedral of St Paul. And when you enter there you see this magnificent painting—Christ at the door knocking.

Someone who saw the painting and later saw Holman Hunt, said, "I didn't see the latch on the door."

"No," he said, "the latch is always on the inside." It has to be opened always from the inside.

We call Jesus the Lord of Lords. We believe that he has all power. "All power has been given to me, in heaven and in earth," he said. He is the King of Kings, he is the Son of God, and yet he stands helpless at the door of the human heart, gently knocking—asking to come in.

Those of us who lived through World War II became altogether too accustomed to the fact that the SS Men of Hitler went to the door of cottage and house and cottage and house. There they would break down the doors, taking large objects and forcing their way in, to find some family that became immediately under arrest and was taken away. They had power and when they were not admitted—and many, many times they were not—they forced their way in. But Jesus, the Christ, stands helpless at the door of the human heart. He does not go where he is not invited. He's always available for the invitation. He never forces his way in—stands there knocking gently at the door, longing to come in. All power! All power! And yet he stands waiting for the latch on the inside to be lifted and the door opens and he is invited in.

Most of you have sung the little song, "Come Into My Heart, Lord Jesus". And most of you have said that to the Christ at some time or another in your life. You've invited him in. You've stood at the altar of a church and said that you loved him, that you would strive to be his follower, that you would read the Scriptures about him and that you would try to apply them to your lives. And you've spoken your vows to God the Father in the name of Jesus Christ. In the Advent season you think of the little baby Jesus in the manger, coming into the world to save the world from its sin. In the Lenten season you think of him there upon his cross bearing the sins of the whole world. And on Easter morning—Glorious Easter! — you think of him alive in the world forevermore.

I'm not asking you for the first time in your lives to accept him, for I think that most of you have. What I want to ask you and me tonight is, "How far into your heart's house have you invited him?" How far—into your heart's house—have you invited him?

Many of you have probably been to or heard of the little town of Camilla, the village where I was born. My father had a number of sisters and a couple of brothers. His mother lived there, my Grandmother Wilson, in the little town. And every Sunday afternoon if it wasn't raining, (we had no automobile, so we had to walk) I'd walk around to the other side of the town to see Grandma. And she was always sitting on the front porch. She was a big woman. I never told her she was. I guess she knew she was but I never tried to remind her that she was. Probably a good thing! But she took up the whole chair and she sat up there on the porch—blind, most of her adult life. I'd run up and kiss Grandma then go across the street and play with Henry Kate Gardner who became my wife. She lived right across the street. I loved to go to Grandma Wilson's house. It was one of those houses that have a hall all the way down the middle of the house—rooms on this side, and rooms on this side. The first door to the left was Grandma's parlor—stayed locked all the time. That bothered me.

That caused me great dismay. And one day I got the courage to ask Grandma, "Why do you keep that door locked all the time?"

She said, "It keeps the likes of you out of it."

So I said, "But who—who goes in that parlor?"

She said, "Well, when the preacher comes, he is invited into the parlor." And I've wondered if that had anything to do with my becoming a preacher— wanting to get into Grandma's parlor. When Grandma died, I remember I was about ten years old, Grandma's casket was in the parlor. It was such a clean room. The rug was so spotless on the floor. There were lace curtains hanging at the two windows. And there was a Grand Piano, one of those old pianos with great legs, over on one side of the room. And there was one of those leather couches that went out this way and came back down that was so comfortable. After Grandma died I lay on it one time. It was a room that she reserved for special people and she always had it clean. So when the preacher came he was not invited into the rest of the house. He was invited into the parlor. When special guests came they were not invited back to Grandma's kitchen; they were invited into the parlor. The rest of the house was all closed off, unless they'd been invited in advance to sit at Grandma's table.

I think that a lot of heart's houses have a parlor, and Jesus comes into this room. I've prepared it for you. I've kept it clean for you. It is a spotless room. And we can have devotions here. And you can sit down here, and I will sit here, and we will have a wonderful visit together. And then when you must go, you will leave the parlor and go out again to find another house where you desire to enter and be entertained.

"O child, don't entertain me in the parlor. Don't limit me to the parlor. Don't tell me that I can go nowhere else in your house except the parlor. I want to go into your house where you **live** your lives. I want to go into the rooms where you yourself use the rooms. And I want to sit down and eat with you. I want an intimacy with you. I want a rich, joyous fellowship with you. Here in this almost too clean a room with lace curtains at the windows and the clean rug on the floor and the spotless walls I don't feel at home because you're not at home here. You keep the door locked. You see you are a stranger to this part of your heart yourself. And you want to hold me here as a prisoner in a clean and spotless but lifeless room. I want to go into your house where you live. I want to sup with you. I want to eat with you."

Hamp said something the other evening about my saying that I thought eating together was one of the most religious things that we could do. And I take that from the fact that Jesus himself frequently sought opportunities to sit down with people and eat with them. He went to Simon's house, and Simon was not one of his, actually. Simon was not noted for his righteousness and all of that, but Jesus sat down with him at his table. He went to Mary and Martha's house and while he fussed at Martha a little bit because she was trying to fix too big a meal, and they didn't really need that big a meal, he sat down with Mary and Martha and ate with them.

And that last night that he was with his disciples in the Upper Room he said, "I have longed to eat the Passover with you." I've wanted to sit around the table with you—where we ate and where we were unhurried, where there was joyous fellowship around the table and where we could speak with each other and share with each other and feel the joy of each other being there. That was the way he spent his last night with the disciples—in that room at a table. We have the wondrous painting that has been reproduced and hangs all over the world—The Last Supper. There he sits in the midst of them, all huddled around, enjoying; with our Lord knowing that it was the last time—sitting together with them around the table.

He didn't take them to the Temple to say, "Let's go in and say our prayers together." He didn't traipse all the way back to Galilee to the mountain where some of them had been with him and feast in the glorious beauty looking down from the mountain where he had been transfigured before them. No, he sat around a simple table with the men that he loved and who in their feeble way loved him, and they had fellowship together.

"Don't, don't keep me up here in this cold room. Don't entertain me up here where you say it's all ready for me. I want to go back into the house where you live."

"Well, Jesus, I'd be glad to have you come into this room, but this is the room in which I count my money. This is the room in which I keep my books. This is the room in which I figure my taxes. This is the room in which I prepare my bills to send out, where I count my money every week. This is **my** room. This is my room. This is my room. I worked hard for it. I have my plans for it. And I haven't thought about your wanting to come in here where everything is so important to **me**—and where it's all mine. Why I'd be grateful if you didn't try to enter this door or ask me to let you in. This is my room."

"Oh friend, I don't want your money. I'm not here to take your money. But you're not enjoying it. You're not enjoying it. You're so scared somebody's going to rob you of it, somebody's going to cheat you out of it, and you sit there anxious becoming gray-haired, worried about what's going to happen to it when you die. You're not happy with it. I'd like to see you happy with it. There's nothing wrong with having it. I'm not against your having it. But I want you to have some joy from having it. I can help you if you'd let me sit down with you and talk about it. We could talk about how God has given it to you, entrusted it to you, and how he has given you a capacity to become so compassionate and loving to reach out with it and have something to share."

"No, Zaccheus, I don't want your money. But you're not enjoying it. And I can help you to walk the streets in Jericho and have every citizen that passes you smile—smile and bow and thank you for your love and integrity and generosity."

"Yes, Master. Yes, Master, come into this room."

"Don't ask to come into this room, Jesus. I, I, I'm sorry. I have a key here hanging around my waist. And it's the key to this room and I can open it, but I'm asking you not to come into this room. This is my room. This is my room. I've been hurt in my life! And I want you to know that. I have been hurt many times in my life. And I want you to know that. And I don't forget 'em. I don't forget them. I do **not** forget them. And I have papered this room; I have papered this room with my hurt and grieving heart. Up there on the wall are:

- all the ugly things that have ever been said to me,
  - the way I've been treated,
    - the way I've been left out,
      - the way I've been neglected, and
        - the way sometimes my family has treated me.

It's all there in the room, and I go in and look at it all. And I think about how it was. And I suffer it all over again. And somehow it seems to help me. Sometimes it seems to fortify me. Sometimes the very bitterness that I feel gives me strength. And this is mine. I don't want you to come in. I don't want you to come in."

"Oh, dear child, you're not happy in that room. You're not happy in that room. Let me come in. We could re-paper this room. We could re-paper this room together. I have some lovely patterns that I could suggest with which you could re-paper this room. Pull down that old paper that has all your hurt and your ill will and your resentment. You can't be happy with all that. God didn't make a heart that could ever be happy with that. Let me come in. That's the very place I want to come in and sit down with you. Let's re-paper it with joy, with loving forgiveness, and with mercy, and with prayers to the Father God that he will forgive you for harboring this so long and robbing yourself of the joy that he could give you. Who knows? Maybe your husband or wife could come home and be "Surprised by the Design" of what we've done and joy could burst out all over this room."

"I don't want to take over the room. I just want you to enjoy this room. Maybe that window that you've shuttered so that there's no sunlight that can get through, you could open wide so that the love of God could fill this room and fill your heart with his love. This is what I want. Don't leave me up in the parlor. Don't force me to stay in that lovely, but cold and lifeless room. Let me come back where you live and help you to find the joy that my Father and I want you to feel. And so before I go, dear child, would you sit with me around the table and we'll hold hands and we'll offer a prayer to our Father God—that he will bless this house, that he will bless this house which is your heart, and that before your life is over every room, every little room will have received his presence and you will know unmistakably his love filling you and giving you his joy.

"Behold I stand at the door and knock." I can't force myself in. And unless you've lifted the latch and let me in, I'm still locked in the parlor. I can't go back into the rest of the house unless I'm invited. I am polite. I am courteous and I wouldn't go invading the intimate parts of your house here and there and here and there unless you invite me. But then we can sit down together and be blessed in each other's fellowship. I will come in and sup with you and be with you forever."

PRAYER

O eternal God and our heavenly Father, forgive us that we've not opened more of ourselves to feel your love revealed to us in Jesus Christ. Help us with these rooms that we've tried too selfishly to keep for ourselves not knowing that if only we invited the Christ into them, they'd be so much more pleasant for us and for any who came to share them with us. And in our lives grant us those blessed times when we seem to sit beside each other and eat together and know the sweetest and dearest fellowship that two can find in each other's presence. We make our prayer in Christ's name and for his sake. Amen.

ETERNAL PROVIDENCE
"Why Doesn't God Do Something?"
Psalms 90:1-4, 16-17, John 5:17 KJV

Wasn't it wonderful to be able to get out of bed this morning? That's what I always try to remember—to be grateful as I think of all the people that can't. How wonderful it is to be able to. For Scripture I choose just one verse from John's Gospel where Jesus has healed the man lying on his bed at the Pool of Bethesda. He says this to justify why he has healed this man on the Sabbath. He says, *"My Father is still working, and I also am working."*

We ask ourselves these turbulent days why God doesn't do something about the world. It looks like every time you pick up the paper something horrible has happened. Sometimes it's way across the world and sometimes it's just across the neighborhood. We had it in Columbus last Thursday. Two members of the Wynnton United Methodist Church, which is one of our fine churches in Columbus, were found in their house. Nobody had heard from them for several days. The Pastor got a call from one of the neighbors, "I don't think things are right."

And so he went with the police over there, and they found the daughter, who was about 55, dead on the floor with a butcher knife left in her chest, and the aged mother who was already helpless clobbered in the bed but still alive somehow. Somebody had gotten into the house and left these two women—one dead and the mother nearly dead. And this kind of thing, you know, strikes you with such horror.

You still read about the Protestants and the Catholics fighting in Ireland, the Palestinians and the Jews in the Mid-east, and such terrible conditions in Africa and you say, "Why doesn't God do something about the world? If I were God I wouldn't put up with all this nonsense." I wouldn't let my children, no parent would let their children run loose like this, carrying arms, hitting one another, and messing up the world. Why doesn't God do something about it? He's powerful. He created the world. He created humankind. He sent his son into the world to try to save it, and it refuses to be saved. Why doesn't he do something?

Sometimes I think he may be sitting up there with Gabriel pretty close by with his horn and Gabriel getting pretty nervous, too, about going ahead and blowing the thing and getting it all over with. And God says, "No, not yet, Gabriel. Not yet."

God is doing something. It's just that God doesn't do things quite the way you and I do. God's doing a great deal across the world that he's not getting credit for and doesn't particularly mind. I want credit for everything I do. I go around putting little "me's" and "my's" and "I's" on so many things that I'd like people to know I did.

I got on the Trailways Bus in Albany one day to go to a meeting in Atlanta. I discovered that I could ride the bus and not have to drive. Somewhere above Leesburg, maybe Smithville, a lady got on the bus and sat down by a lady who was sitting in front of me. When two ladies get together and haven't anything else to do, they start talking about recipes, I discovered. And I discovered that when they get to talking about recipes it isn't long before they start sharing their pound cake recipes. I don't know why pound cake is such a big thing, but it is. So these two got to talking about pound cake. One decided she would give her recipe to the other. She had a good, bold, strong voice. And I'm sure we all could have taken down the recipe on the bus if we had had a mind to.

But she went like this, "First, I take my sugar, and then I take my butter." Now don't take this down because it's not the recipe, but this is the way she was giving it out.

"Then I take my flour, then I take my eggs, then I take my vanilla," and whatever else you put in it, it was all "mine". I take my eggs and my sugar and my flour and my butter. Why not just take eggs and take butter? **My** eggs and **My** butter and **My** flour. Well, they were hers, I'm sure. She bought them at the store.

But we just keep going this way from childhood, right on into our old age—"That's mine. That's mine. That's mine."

Being the preacher, I know it happens to me every time I go to a dinner on the ground or covered dish. People are so nice to preachers—always wanting us to have the best. And you know that woman who's sure that she always brings the best of everything. "Now that's my lemon pie right over there. I sure want you to have a slice of **my** lemon pie."

You go to the fair. I've been to the fair a lot of times. You go to the livestock competition and there's a man standing there. "That's my cow," he says, "My cow."

Well, we just do that all the time. God doesn't. God doesn't. You go out into your rose garden this morning, if you're still fortunate enough to have some roses, and there may be the loveliest bloom in all the wide, wide world. And as if it weren't enough to have all this loveliness in the blossom there are three or four little diamonds of dew right on top of it to crown it. And you look around for a tag to see whose it is. Who did this? You won't find a tag on it—"This is my rose!"—Signed "God". You won't find that. "I created this rose."—Signed "God". "P. S., and don't you forget it." You won't find that. But he's out there in his world creating all this loveliness and this beauty, just as quietly.

Sunday, two of my members told me of having gone up into New England already and they've come back home again. And they said, "Frederick, you just don't believe it. You can't believe it unless you go. We have color, but we don't have color like that." All these yellows and all these reds, all these gorgeous colors of the leaves in New England and you just ride and ride and it's just one great portrait of color. And how did it all change? Were there any bands playing? Did God demand a parade the day he was going to change the colors of all the leaves? If you held a microphone up to those leaves when it was happening could you hear anything when they were changing from green to yellow to red? Not a sound. Not a proclamation anywhere around. God just painting the world red and yellow and no demand for anyone to come and look.

One morning we were in Albany leaving early to visit Lake Junaluska. We left Albany I guess about 5:30 in the morning with my wife and the three girls on the back seat. Somewhere just this side of Americus the sun began to rise and the five of us had never seen the sun rise at the same time. We'd seen it at different times, some of us coming in and some of us going out. But we'd never all seen the sun rise at one time. And it began to happen there. It was so magnificent that I pulled the car off the road, and there on the shoulder we sat for about five minutes and watched this thing. It was the most glorious sunrise I ever saw in Georgia. Oh this portrait on the Eastern horizon—absolutely magnificent! Just enough clouds to give it all kinds of interest, all the different shades of pink and lavender and purple. We just sat there breathless and silent. And one of the little girls said, "Does this happen every morning?"

"Every morning." And not a single time has God entered any house and taken anybody by the shoulders to say, "Get up, I'm about the make the sun rise. I want somebody out there to see it. And I'm not going to let it rise until there's somebody out there to see it. I want at least a thousand people and I'm not going to let it rise until I have a thousand to witness it." God never ever shook my shoulder to say, "Come see my sunrise! That's mine." God just works so quietly, so unostentatiously, but working just the same.

Out in New Guinea several of the sailors and I who were stationed at a hospital there found the afternoons to be sometimes quiet. We didn't have many patients. We were so far behind the lines. There were a lot of us and we really weren't doing very much. You remember, I think, Churchill said at Dunkirk, wasn't it, that, "Never have so few done so much for so many." Well out there we said, "Never have so many done so little for so few." And that was sort of what we were doing. So one afternoon we climbed up a hill. We'd never been up that way. Beautiful country out there, actually, and at one point we had to get down on our hands and knees to go under some low trees. Suddenly we came into a clearing, and there in front of us was a tree. It turned out to be a hibiscus tree and it was in full red bloom.

I'd never seen one so large. I had never seen such a magnificent thing of beauty. It was like one of our Dogwood trees except that it all was red.

We were there on our hands and knees and one of the boys, when he saw it, gasped, "God!" I didn't know whether it was a word of praise or whether it was an expletive or what, but it was the right word—"God!" Don't you know that if I had been making that tree I would have wanted it at Five Points, Atlanta, or somewhere on one of the busy avenues of New York with a great big flag waving over it, "This is mine. God!" But not God. Just works quietly away. Jesus said in John's Gospel, *"My father worketh hitherto, and I work."* They just don't work like we do. We want credit all the time. We want people to know what we've done. We want to see it ourselves and we want to sign our names to it and we want to make sure that everybody else understands that we've been doing something worthwhile.

But not God. He's quietly working away in His world with people like you, people like you. He doesn't put tags on you when you're going around quietly doing his work for him. You never found one when you got up in the morning hanging around your neck—"This is mine." Signed, "God." He just sends you out to do what he wants you to do, what he needs you to do. He doesn't advertise you. He doesn't put your names in the eternal Gazette. He just sends you out quietly to do it. He didn't have any bands playing when the church was erected over there, any parades marching up and down the street. Just quietly go about the doing of his will in the world.

Oh all this evil does bother us though. Why don't you do something about it, God? All these wicked people, people that are not like us, people that just do these terrible things. Why don't you do something about them? God says, "I'm doing something about them. You want it done today. I don't mind about today. I've thousands and thousands and thousands of years. I'm in no hurry. You all are in a hurry. You've got to get it done today. You said you won't be here tomorrow."

When we turn sixty, we begin to feel that way. I need to get it done. I won't be around. God says, "I'll be around. I'll be around." A thousand years is just as yesterday, said the Psalmist. God's got all the time in the world. And he'll get it done.

We stood one day in Rome on our way back from the Holy Land where we'd had a wonderful tour. The guide took us to the site of some building there in Rome and he said, "Right up there is the balcony from which Mussolini did most of his speaking in Rome. He stood there and he spoke to the people." I've heard that voice on the radio. Did you hear the voice of Mussolini on the radio? Oh, Dear God, it was enough to frighten you to death just coming over the radio. Loud! Threatening—going to take over the world! He meant it and he started out doing it.

The guide said, "Do you know what we call that balcony now? We call it The Balcony of Bad Memories." You can go throughout the whole city of Rome where Mussolini stood with such threatening power one day to assert himself before the world and there's not one thing in the whole city of Rome that bears the name of Mussolini. Not one thing. Took down every sign. No little alley named for him—nothing anywhere. "I'll take care of him," said God. "Don't you worry about him. He'll have his little say. He'll walk across the stage. He'll assert himself and then he's gone. Gone forever."

One of my memories of being at Emory in the early morning was of a few of us sitting around on the floor listening to the radio. That was the big thing when we were coming along. We were listening to the voice of Hitler coming across the world. Oh that voice was even more threatening. It was a raucous, ugly voice. He would scream out that he was going to take the world and he meant to take the world, and he near about did. There were some people that thought he was. Threatening the world. Six million Jews, they tell us, just went into evaporation—cruel bestial evaporation under the power of this man. Where is he now? Still hanging by his neck somewhere, gone. Gone, gone, gone forever. One great big bad memory, a few pages of the history book, and he's gone. God says, "Don't worry, I'm doing something. I'm just not under the pressure of time like you are. I'll get it done. Don't you worry about that. My world is still my world. And my will will be done in my world. Just don't expect me to do it the same way you would do it if you momentarily had the power to do it."

So you see it takes giant faith to believe this. If you did nothing today but to read the headlines in the morning paper, to listen to the 8 o'clock news, and just focus on the bad things happening across the world, you'd have no choice but to despair. You'd say, "Well what's the use trying? Why should I try to do good with all this terrible evil all across the world?" It would be so easy to despair. It is for so many people. What's the use?

Well, there's a lot of use. There's a lot of use. With a giant faith we believe this is God's world. This is My Father's World. And things will come out right.

You remember that day. You weren't there. You've been there in spirit. They hung a good, perfect, wonderful man on a cross. And it looked like the whole jig was over. That's what all the people standing around the cross were thinking— "Well we nailed him there. That's it." These over here saying, "We put him there and that's it. We won't hear from him again. Dead men don't bless and dead men don't heal and dead men don't teach. Dead men are just dead." But he wasn't dead. He came quietly one morning back into the world.

Don't you know that if I had been God I would have wanted at least a thousand trumpets that Easter Morning to announce that he was coming back into the world? Just as quiet as that rose is blooming there this morning, Jesus stepped out into the world again, and the first word that he spoke was to one little woman that was in the garden. "Mary," he said, just that quiet, just that still, "Mary." That's what he said when he came back. No, he wasn't dead. It looked mighty gloomy on that Friday. But now we call it "Good" Friday because out of it God brought his Son back into the world and he is still here. It takes a giant faith to believe that and to keep right on persevering and doing the good you're doing and being the kind, compassionate person you are, making your little contribution to the good of God's world, because that good is going to triumph.

You may not see it. You may not live to see the world a rose garden, a paradise. But it is God's world. "He's working," says Jesus, "and I'm working." So let us work, too, daring to believe that one day the Kingdom of our God will be also the Kingdom of this earth.

PRAYER

Father God, we pray for that kind of faith. Some days it's mighty hard for us not to despair about the condition of the world. Help us to keep knowing it is your world and that you will bring your will to bear in it. Give us this kind of simple, believing but sturdy faith in your greatness and goodness as God our Father. Bless us all day long. In Christ's name. Amen.

TRANSFIGURATION
"Discouragement Transfigured"
I Kings 19:1-18, Luke 9:28-36 KJV

The passage that I would like to read is in Luke's Gospel. It's in the ninth chapter, and it's Luke's account of the transfiguration. And Luke tells us something about that experience of the Christ on the mountaintop with the three disciples that went along with him so often on very important missions—Peter, James and John. He tells us about the purpose of Jesus in going to the mountain. He was indeed transfigured before the disciples. They saw him in a light in which they had never been able to see him before. Though Peter had said that he was indeed the Christ, there on the mountain he saw the amazing quality and character of this Christ whom he had pledged to support with all of his loyalty and devotion.

These three, Peter, James and John, who were the leaders of the group, would have fixed in their own minds that this was indeed the Christ, the Son of the Living God. When he was no longer with them in the flesh, this spiritual experience that they had with him would let them know in a giant kind of way that he was still alive with them and that they should not fear. But in addition, Luke says, a part of the reason for his going to the top of the mountain was *"To speak of his death which he should accomplish at Jerusalem."* And there appeared out of spirit world two figures—Moses and

Elijah, who came down out of spirit world and ministered to the Christ as he was there on the mountaintop contemplating what already seemed to be so clearly known to him as his destiny. And that was his own death. Luke says in verses 30 and 31, *"There talked with him two men which were Moses and Elijah who appeared in glory and spoke of his death which he should accomplish in Jerusalem."*

I take it that Jesus wasn't ready to die. I take it that he wasn't ready to begin to think about dying. And I think he realized his need to find himself in the presence of his Father God who would arrange for him a spirit experience. He needed to be assured by his Father God that his death, which was imminent, would indeed accomplish God's purpose through him.

I think Jesus was discouraged. He hadn't accomplished a great deal. He didn't have a great deal to show for what he had done. He had called this little band of men, but they were so weak, they were so frail, they were so lacking in understanding. They didn't really know what he was about. They didn't comprehend the bigness of his mission. And he already had so many enemies who followed him about asking all kinds of catchy questions and doing everything they could to ensnare and entrap him. And he had so much that he wanted to accomplish:
- so many things that he wanted to do,
  - so many people that he wanted to reach,

- so many more parables that he wanted to tell,
  - so many more miracles that he wanted to perform.

And the cross looms large on the horizon of his life. And I think he was discouraged.

And I think that's part of the reason, and Luke says it's true that he went to the mountaintop, as he was accustomed to do. There God opened spirit world and down came the wonderful spirit of Moses and the wondrous spirit of Elijah to minister to the discouraged spirit of Jesus the Christ.

I don't think we take advantage of spirit world, as we ought. All of us know some mighty wonderful people who are a part of spirit world. Oh I don't mean we should get in semi-darkened rooms and have all kinds of strange noises going and all kinds of lights doing mysterious and frightening things and call down out of spirit world someone to speak to us. I don't mean anything of this kind. But I mean the quiet remembering of some very wonderful people that are now a part of spirit world who were a part of our worlds. They walked with us a little while and touched our lives and blessed them. Every now and again we ought to make it a part of our devotional lives to call down the spirit of someone that we knew and loved to minister to us in our times of discouragement.

This is the one great temptation Satan uses, I think, on people like you and me. The devil works on all of us in all kinds of ways. He never leaves us alone. And the temptation with which he is constantly battling me is discouragement, discouragement. Now you all remember so very well when that argument broke loose and the shocking words were announced that there was a professor at Emory University that said God is dead. All that's passed us now. We lived through that. I kept praying that somebody would announce that the Devil was dead, but nobody ever announced it. Nobody ever dared to say that the Devil was dead. He is **not** dead. And he comes constantly knocking at the doors of our minds and spirits offering us any conceivable thing that he can to ensnare and entrap us.

And discouragement is the thing that he comes to me with. "What do you think you're really accomplishing?" This is what he says. Particularly on Sunday night and I'm lying in my bed trying to go to sleep remembering some of the faults of the day, the poverty of the sermon. He says to me, "Now just what do you think you're accomplishing? Tomorrow how many people will remember what you preached anyway? And I dare you that next Sunday, after you've preached, you could stand at the door of the church and every tenth person that comes out you could ask 'What did I preach about?' and they couldn't tell you five minutes after you had preached what you had preached about. Why don't you quit? Why don't you get on my side? Why don't you get with the winning team?" And I think that this is what he was after with Jesus, just discouragement.

And so, out of spirit world God sent Moses and Elijah. Why did he send Moses? Why did he send Elijah? I know Moses represents the law and Elijah represents prophecy. I know all about that. But I have some very personal reasons why I think he chose these particular two. He had a whole realm from which to choose. There are some wonderful people up there, or wherever they are. He had Hosea and he had Micah and he had Abraham. He had all kinds of wonderful people that he could have chosen. He chose Moses. He chose Elijah.

"Jesus, this is Moses. You remember me?"

"Oh yes, Moses, I read your story innumerable times from the scroll in the little synagogue at Nazareth. You're a great man, Moses—an enviable leader of our people, and I've always admired you."

"Oh but, Jesus, there was a time. There was a time when things weren't so well with me. Do you recall reading about the day God told me to come up on the mountain and standing there on the mountain he said to me, 'Moses, there it is! See it? That's the Promised Land. That's the destination of my people. That's where they will settle down and a nation will be born. They will be my people and I will be their God. There it is Moses. See it on the horizon. Within sight, Moses, that's the Promised Land.'

Oh, I cried out, thank you, God. Thank You, God. Thank you, God, for bringing me to this moment where I know that it is not only a possibility but a reality that I will lead this people into the Promised Land.

'Oh no, Moses,' God said to me, 'you will not lead them into the Promised Land. You will never set foot in that Promised Land.'

Oh no, God, I cried. Where is your justice, God? It was I that you found on the mountain at the burning bush. It was I that you persuaded against my better judgment to go to Egypt to lead this people. It was I who stood up to Pharoah. It was I who led them out of that land. It was I who suffered through all of their weaknesses and their frailties in the wilderness. And now you tell me, now you tell me that I will not enter this Promised Land with this people.

'No, Moses. I needed you to get it all started. I needed you to plant the seed. I don't necessarily need you to be there for the harvest. I needed you to begin it for me. And I needed you to carry it for me a long long time, which you've done, but I don't need you to complete it, Moses. You don't have to see it completed. But believe me, it will be completed. Thank you, Moses for the part you've done. Now others will see it completed. But have no fear, Moses. Feel no discouragement, Moses. Your people will enter the Promised Land.'"

I'm like Moses. Anything I start I want to see finished. Anything I have anything to do with I want to see completed. Any seed I plant I want to see come up. And I want to eat the fruit off of the things that come up that I've planted. I'm that much like Moses.

I'm that much like you. I'm that much like thousands and thousands of other people who hesitate to plant a seed if they think they're not going to be there to reap the harvest from the planting of the seed.

So a lot of people quit when they think they're not going to get in on the harvest. A lot of people get greatly discouraged when they don't see the results begin to take place that they think by now ought to be taking place. It may not have happened in this church, but in some church this very week some Sunday School teacher went to the Sunday School Superintendent or the pastor to say, "I'm not getting anywhere with these boys and girls. They're not responding to me. I don't seem to be accomplishing anything. I'd appreciate it very much if you'd just get another teacher. I don't think I'll ever, ever be able to reach them." And the Devil's gotten to her and just discouraged her. Didn't make an adulteress out of her. Didn't make an alcoholic out of her. Didn't make a thief out of her. Didn't make a murderess out of her. Just discouraged her—that's all. Just convinced her that she wasn't accomplishing anything. Just convinced her that the seed she was planting would never bear fruit. And so she asked out. She asked to quit because she was discouraged.

"Oh, Jesus," Moses said, "God doesn't necessarily require you to be around when his will is ultimately achieved. You don't have to see all these things take place. You don't have to reach all the people. You don't have to perform all the miracles; you don't have to tell all the parables. You just do what God wants you to do—the one thing God wants you to do. You just do that and trust God to see it through. Trust God to complete it. Trust God to bring it to its final fruition, its destiny and its destination."

Oh, Dear God, if I can remember that. If I can only learn that as a part of my Christian life—God wants me to plant the seed. It doesn't matter to him whether I'm around to see the harvest. There will be a harvest! Those little seeds I plant somewhere in somebody's heart may come to life one day.

A white haired woman told me not a month ago about a letter in her desk drawer. She was a schoolteacher. And some student 25 years later was writing her the grateful thanks that he should have expressed. He was apologizing in the letter for not expressing it at the time. But he said, "For 25 years I've carried in my mind something that you told me one afternoon after school about my life."

This dear white haired lady sat in that chair, now a near invalid for a decade wondering if she'd ever done any good, if she'd ever really helped a life, if she'd ever really added anything on the plus side to the lives of people whose lives had touched hers. And then came the blessed letter. Yes the seed you planted has come to life in a man who pauses gratefully to thank you for the seed you planted in his life.

We don't have to be around. We don't have to see the job completed. God just says to us, "Get it started for me. Do something for me. Get it on its way and then trust me to bring it to full fruition." You remember when Jesus was hanging on the cross? Those were the last words that he said. He said,

"Father, I entrust it to you." And that's what Moses was asking him to do. "Say, 'Father, I entrust it to you.'" In full confidence that his Father God would take his spirit and with it would change a world!

"Jesus, this is Elijah. Do you remember me?"

"O yes, Elijah, I remember you. How many times I have read of your wonderful life from the scroll in the synagogue in our little village of Nazareth. O, Elijah, you were a great man. You were a bold man. And how I envied you many times as a child—that boldness in your life."

"Oh but, Jesus, that was the most humiliating day of my life. Do you remember? I almost hope you don't remember—the day I was lying on my stomach in a cave, beating the floor of that cave with my fists crying out of my anguish, Oh God, let me die. Let me die. I'm the only man in the world that seems to care about anything that's good. I'm the only person left in the world that seems to care about you, God. All of them have gone to the dogs. All of them have run away. There's no one really faithful. And it's too big a job for anybody. Just let me die, Lord. Just let me die! Oh Jesus, I'm embarrassed to tell you about it, but that's the way it was.

And God came into that cave and found me there lying on my stomach beating my fists against the stone floor of the cave and he said, 'Elijah, what are you doing here? I asked you to do one thing, Elijah. I didn't ask you to take the whole world on your shoulders and try to run it. I'm not holding you responsible for the whole world. I gave you one job

to do. I told you to go back one more time to the
palace of that wicked King and Queen. And I told
you to stand in front of them one more time and say,
"Thus saith the Lord God!" He has a will for you
whether you are King or Queen or what. He has a
will for you. That's all I asked you to do Elijah. I
haven't asked you to take on your shoulders and on
your heart the whole world. I've asked you to do one
thing. And here you are lying on the floor of the cave
as if you're responsible for the whole world. And
because it doesn't seem to you to be going just the
way you would like it to go you think there's no
reason any longer to live. Well, I'll tell you a little
secret. I have a few more people beside you who still
know my name. I have a few who are still faithful to
me. Get up off that floor, Elijah, and go do the one
thing I asked you to do.'"

I can remember nights when it seemed to me
during those rather crucial and tense and
terrible days in Albany that I was responsible for the
whole race problem of the world. It seemed to settle
down on my heart and on my shoulders that I was
responsible for the whole civil rights movement. I
was responsible for all the racial tensions of the
world. Lying there in my bed sleepless and feeling
that the whole thing was hopeless. And that some
way I was responsible for the whole thing and that
God was holding me responsible for the whole thing.
I can remember nights after the 11 o'clock News
when I still sat in the chair feeling that I was
responsible for all of Watergate, the whole thing.

Because it was my nation, because it was my President, I was responsible for the whole thing. It weighed down on my mind and on my spirit like a ton. Like a ton dropped on it. And I felt the whole world was evil, the whole thing is wretched and unbearable and the only thing to do is just to get out of it. And God has been trying to say to me, "I put you at St. Paul. I didn't put you in the whole world. I put you at St. Paul. And I ask you to pastor the people of St. Paul. I didn't ask you to take over the city of Washington. I asked you to be the shepherd of the people at St. Paul. Do you think you can manage that?"

Yes, Father. Yes, Father.

"Well leave the world to me. Leave Washington to me. It may seem a hopeless situation, but one day, one day, I am your God and your Father. I'll work out my world. I'll work out your nation. All I'm asking of you is to work in that little vineyard where I placed you. You think you can do that?"

Yes, Father. I think I can.

"Well, Jesus, that's what God was trying to say to me," concluded Elijah in that wonderful moment that they had together on the top of the mountain. God said to poor old Elijah, "Elijah, I'm not holding you responsible for the world. But I gave you a job to do, and I want you to go do it."

"And Oh, Jesus, I got up off the floor of that cave and I ran to that wicked King and that Queen that sat beside him more wicked than he, and I said in the best voice I could muster, 'Thus saith the Lord

God.' I did the thing God asked **me** to do and left the rest to God."

"So Jesus, your Father is not asking you to convert the world. He's not asking you to go to every nation of the world. He's not asking you to take upon your shoulders all the wickedness and evil of the world. He's asking you to give yourself completely through your will to him to be used this time."

So he stretched himself at last upon the cross and did the one great thing God sent him into the world to do.

So now you see on a Sunday night lying there still worried about the sermon of the day and still maybe a little discouraged about how little I seem to be contributing to it all, he comes again. He never gives up. And he taps me on the shoulder and he says to me, "Just what do you think you accomplished today?" And Jesus has given me an answer. I say, "Listen, Devil. You go ask my Father. I don't know what I did today. You go ask him. Because maybe, just maybe this very day I did something for my Father that 25 years from now may prove to be a miracle."

So:

- When he comes again with all the headlines blaring as they always do with all the wickedness and evil in the world that breaks our hearts and sends us into despair that we could be part of a race that could be so cruel and so inhuman,

- When we feel like it's just too much and the only thing to do is to get out of it,
- And when the Devil comes and says, "Why don't you?" "Why don't you?"

I remember, and I say to him, "Devil, God has given me St. Paul, and in the morning I'll be back there doing the best I can with the one thing God has entrusted to me."

So God has helped me with my battle against discouragement. Jesus faced it and he overcame it magnificently. And he is our help, he is our strength, he is our inspiration. And on the journey that we make, he is our companion who keeps saying to us, "Don't be discouraged! Don't be discouraged! God will take the little bit that you bring in your hands and make a miracle."

**Dr. Frederick Wilson baptizing Carleton Walker Fry, Jr.
At St. Paul United Methodist Church , Columbus, Ga.
December, 1979**

BROADMINDED?
"Broadminded But Shallow"
Matthew 7:13 KJV

I haven't read this passage of Scripture aloud in a service of worship in a long time. Maybe that's a sin of omission on my part, because increasingly now I feel the need to read it silently myself and to read it aloud more times than I have. It's in the Sermon on the Mount. It's in the seventh chapter of Matthew and it's verse 13 and a verse or two following. *"Enter ye in at the strait gate"* and that's strait, STRAIT, not straight, STRAIGHT—the strait gate, and strait means hard, difficult. *"Enter ye in at the strait gate, for wide is the gate and broad is the way that leadeth to destruction, and many there be which go in thereat. Because strait is the gate—* hard, difficult, *—and narrow is the way that leadeth unto life and few there be that find it."*

I was at Emory a long, long time ago. When I was at Emory, the big word was broad-minded. That was really a big word. It was the big ideal, apparently. Be broad in your understanding of things. Be broad in your acceptance of things. Be broad in your sympathies and in your compassion. And broad-minded was a kind of an ideal. Don't be narrow. Don't be little. Don't be provincial. Don't be local. Be big! Be broadminded. And it was an ideal and it became one of my ideals. I didn't want to be a little preacher—a little thinking preacher. I didn't want to be a narrow preacher.

Some of you this week have mentioned Brother Bascomb Anthony. Let me tell you one of the stories that I remember about Dr. Anthony, and there were of course innumerable ones because he was so unique and so completely an individual. He was over at Thomasville and was serving there and one of his very dear friends was Dr. Calloway who was the pastor of First Baptist Church. And the Baptists were going to entertain the Georgia Baptist Convention. And they were getting homes where the delegates could stay. You know there were no motels and that kind of thing in that day. And one day Dr. Anthony said to Dr. Calloway, "Well, I hear you're looking for homes for your Baptist delegates. Well, Mrs. Anthony and I will take 25."

"Twenty-five!" said Dr. Calloway. "Where in the world are you going to put twenty-five?"

"Well," said Brother Bascomb, "As narrow as you Baptists are, we can sleep that many here at our house." And every now and then we call our Baptist friends a little narrow and they don't like it and we shouldn't say it, actually, but Dr. Anthony could say it and I guess get by with it.

But we don't like narrow. We don't like little. We don't like provincial. We don't like local. We want to be broad. We want to be big. And so the word was a very, very ideal word for me. And it was a kind of objective and goal to achieve—to be a broad-minded person and to be a broad-minded minister.

My first assignment in the South Georgia Conference was as Conference Youth Director. I lived in Macon, traveled all over the Conference trying to help organize youth groups and encourage the ones already organized that weren't doing so well and all that kind of thing. I had a service station that I used in Macon. I liked Bob very much. He was the man in charge. And it was the time when the war in Europe was beginning to be a great threat and things in America were beginning to be a little bit severe. And automobile tires were rationed. I guess some of you remember that. And one day I pulled up into the service station and got some gas and Bob came around and he said, "How about signing the form I have in here to get four tires."

I said, "Bob, I don't need any tires. I'm fortunate. I'm ready for the rationing because my tires are in good shape."

He said, "I know that, but I have a friend who needs some tires real bad and you're on a list. You can get tires. Ministers can apply for tires and get them. And I'd be mighty glad if you would sign the form to get the tires and I could sell 'em to my friend who needs 'em real bad."

I said, "Bob, uh, I don't think I could do that. I don't believe that would be right—for me to sign a form saying that I needed tires as a minister for my work and then when the tires arrived, I'd turn them over to you to sell to your friend. I just don't believe I can do that."

And I nearly fell out of the car when he said to me, "Oh, Preacher, be broad-minded." Well, there was my word. It really did shock me, severely, because there was my word—my big star in the sky that I wanted to be the beacon to guide me to be this big, broad understanding person with a breadth of interests and sympathies and compassions and all this. And here is that word. Somehow it's not a good word anymore. Broadminded means that I'm supposed to surrender my idea of what integrity is and what honor is and what honesty is, and put my name to a document which is a lie. That's what it would be, actually, because I would not be telling the truth. And I began to understand that that's what broadminded meant to a lot of people.

I joined the Navy as a Chaplain and my first overseas assignment was in Brisbane, Australia and I was attached to a submarine repair unit. It was built hurriedly alongside the river there and we used some old wool warehouses for our quarters. The submarines would come in from the 7th Fleet and the crew would go on a two-week leave up into one of the lovely sections of Australia and our crew would take over and get everything in order so that they could go out again when they came back.

But whenever they came in, and it seemed to me that they came in mighty often, there would be a party at our little quarters for the crew and for the officers. The crew had theirs one place and the officers had theirs at another. And as I say, it seemed to me that there were too many of those parties. But they always had, you know, plenty to drink at those parties. I would go to the parties because it was an opportunity to meet the officers. I could find out if there were some things that they needed on the submarine that I could get for them—some books or games or this kind of thing, or if there were any men particularly that had any problems. They might have had some news from home that was not good and I might see them when they came back.

So I was there at the parties. And there was one of our crew, Cooky, who every time they had a party insisted that I have a drink. I mean, you know, an alcoholic drink. And I said, "Cooky, uh, I just don't drink, never have, and I don't see any point in starting now."

"Oh come on, have a drink, not gonna' hurt you."

"No, no."

Next party he'd come up again. "Padre, have a drink."

"No, Cooky, I don't really care for one."

"Well, Man, it's 3000 miles from home. Who's ever gonna know you had a drink?" And he would argue.

Well the next time, he'd say, "Have a drink."

And I'd say, "Cooky, what day of the week is this?"

He said, "Tuesday".

I said, "Tuesday, I never drink on Tuesday." I had just decided to go along with him.

And one day, you know, he said, "Have a drink. Come on now, have a drink. You'll enjoy it. You'll like it."

I said, "No, Cooky, I just never have done that and don't particularly care…"

"Oh, Padre, why in the (Expletive) can't you be broadminded?"

There my word was again. Traveled halfway around the world and there my word was— broadminded. And what it means is just forget what you've tried to live up to over the years. Just forget the principles of morality that you've tried to practice in your life. Let your ideals come way on down low. And I think we're in grave danger here in our country now of this kind of thing happening to all of us.

We compare ourselves to some who are so much worse, and this is possible for all of us. You think of Watergate and all that and you think of all the evil that exists all across the world, and then you say, "Well I'm not so bad. Oh it doesn't really matter particularly if I do this or if I do that." And before we are aware of it, we have surrendered some ideal. We have broadened our life, but we have made it shallow at the same time. Jesus said broad is the way that leads to destruction and many, many find that way. But narrow is the way that leadeth unto life.

We haven't liked that word narrow. Great tennis players like that word narrow. And great musicians like that word narrow. And they live by that word narrow. My first year of college I met Billy Pardee over at Valdosta. And Billy's been kind of an inspiration to me across the years, because he played the violin. His mother played the violin. His mother taught violin in the college at Valdosta.

And Billy was determined to be a great violinist. Well, I don't think he's captured honors all over the world, but even at 19 he was a brilliant violinist.

"Well," Billy said, "you know, this doesn't just happen." And he told me about afternoon after afternoon after afternoon that he'd hear his playmates outside. He was a little boy. And then he was a youth, which was even more difficult. He'd hear them playing outside. He'd hear them calling to him. But the great big doors had swung shut to his living room and Billy was inside with his violin hour after hour after hour. Out there were all these other things that he would have liked to do, and all of these other activities in which he would like to engage, and where he would have been a perfect fit, and where he would have had some skill, I'm sure, and where he would have made many, many more friends than he had. But he had dedicated himself to learning that violin, so he closed the doors. And he would stay there with it. And life narrows itself down to something that a person wants to achieve in and to achieve greatly in. And life becomes tremendously narrow for that person—tremendously narrow!

That's what Jesus was talking about. But it leads to life. I mean it leads to something tremendous. It leads to something satisfying—soul satisfying, mind satisfying. And while on the surface of it we don't like the word narrow, it's the word narrow when we apply it to our lives that leads to something which is of tremendous significance.

So this is what Jesus is talking about with reference to the moral life. You can't just do anything you want to. You can't just follow any whim or desire that happens to suggest itself to your mind. You understand that life is filled with choices and that Almighty God has honored us by giving us the capacity, the free will, to make our own choices. And we can make them. We can make them. And we can begin to make them in small ways; "Oh this won't hurt." Or, "This won't make much difference." Or, "Nobody will ever know if I do this." And before very long that principle of free choice has begun to operate and it sort of multiplies until before one knows it, it doesn't really matter what one does. And one can do it, you know, with a sort of a glib mind and a kind of casual spirit. This is what Jesus is talking about here. "Broad is the way that leads to destruction and many, many go in by that way."

I was reading last night for a little while Barclay's Commentary on the Epistle to the Romans and in the early chapters of the Letter to the Romans Paul writes that God has abandoned certain men. And Barclay says that this is a terrible word, "Abandoned". You just desert it. You just walk away from it. You just leave it. That God has abandoned certain men? Yes, because that was the choice **they** made. They just started out that way. "It doesn't really matter what I do. It doesn't matter if I do this. It doesn't matter if I do that." And before long this has become a way of life. And instead of choosing anything that's good or moral or upright or honorable, they choose the opposites. And this becomes the way of life. And it isn't that God abandons, Barclay said. **They** have abandoned God. And the way of life that they have chosen has simply eliminated God altogether from their lives. Narrow is the way that leadeth unto life.

We don't want to be ugly narrow. We don't want to be the kind of people that are intolerant and intolerable because we are pious or because we are so good. This is not good. This doesn't attract people. There's nothing warm or inviting about this. But at long last there has to be some kind of moral standard by which we live so that we are respected. At long last people do not judge people who are Christ's by what we say but by what we are. And while I think that Cooky wanted me to take a drink, if Cooky had ever come in and found me at the end of one of those parties a little too UN-sober, I think even Cooky would not have respected me. And I don't think that he would have ever sat down to talk with me about some tremendous longing of his own heart. Or if he had received news from home that his wife had died suddenly that he would have particularly cared to search me out, expecting that I would offer him sympathy or compassion or hope. I think that though he might have been the one that wanted to sort of push me a little and nudge me a little into doing something that would momentarily have given him a little comfort because the "Chaplain" was doing it, I think ultimately that he would have had no respect for me and would have shared nothing of his heart with me.

One of the places I went in the Navy, and I learned a great deal in the Navy, I replaced a Chaplain that was not very popular on the base—not at all. This was up in New Guinea. It was dull up there where we were—nothing going on of any significance and the officers played a lot of poker and the Chaplain played poker with them. That was his undoing. He wasn't a very good poker player. He should have known he wasn't a very good poker player. Chaplains aren't good poker players. He should have stayed in his little Quonset hut. He should have never gotten involved in it. He got in debt to **all** of the officers. This was literally the case. And I came aboard and got to know several of them and I said, "You played poker with Chaplain Fink didn't you?"

"Yes."

I said, "Did you take communion from him?"

"No! Hell, No!"

This happens to us. We think we can sort of play around with it and it won't do any harm particularly and it won't make a great deal of difference. But ere long we know that people aren't trusting us, that people aren't really believing our profession. The broadmindedness that we sort of wanted to achieve and accomplish in our lives has destroyed something that was very precious and very dear and very vital to us. We can be broadminded. But so often in the process we become shallow.

One of my childhood memories was my mother making chocolate fudge. She had a platter that she poured it out in that was this big. I never saw such a dish. It was made to hold a very big turkey or a little pig; I'm not sure which. But it was a great big dish. And mother would pour it out and then she would just spread it fast. I could see her just going with it. And then she'd cut it. And then she'd say, "Now you can have two pieces," as if she were giving you the world. And you'd take two pieces, and bless me, it would be so thin, when you got it in your mouth you didn't have anything. You have a broad big old platter of chocolate fudge, but it's so shallow you don't get anything when you get it. And that's the way with a lot of folks. Just so broadminded that they're shallow too. And of the two words narrow and shallow, I guess I'd rather be narrow than shallow.

One Sunday at Statesboro I did try to develop this subject, and so Monday morning out on the bulletin board I just put those words, Broadminded but Shallow. When I came in at Noon, Henry Kate said, "I think you had better go check the bulletin board."

And I said, "Oh, did the secretary misspell Broadminded?"

She said, "You just go check the bulletin board."

So I went out and checked the bulletin board. I came back and I said, "Everything's spelled right."

She said, "You'd better go check again." She said, "Start at the top and read right down."

So I went outside and I read,

> STATESBORO FIRST METHODIST CHURCH
> J. FREDERICK WILSON, PASTOR
> BROADMINDED BUT SHALLOW

"Oh," I said, "Now I'm announcing it to the whole community."

Broad is the way that leadeth to destruction and many go in thereat, but narrow is the way that leadeth unto life. Let's be among the few that find it.

Prayer

Father God, we thank you for this new day and for the joy that we've had in being here together in this warm fellowship this morning. How we thank you for our love for one another and the sense of belonging that we feel within the arms of the church, and within your loving care. Bless us all day long. Use us in your service. We pray in Christ's name. Amen.

TEMPTATION
"Lead Us Not Into Temptation"
Matthew 4:1-11, 6:13 KJV

I want to talk about temptation this morning. I don't understand, and don't guess any of us does, why there is so much evil in the world. But the world seemed to have gotten started with evil in it. God himself didn't explain to Adam and Eve why it was there. Actually, he didn't warn them that it was there, just placed them in this paradise and there they lived a while. But it wasn't long before they discovered that there was temptation. And then they discovered the dire consequences of their yielding to the power of the evil in the world.

Their two children were born. I don't know of a more pathetic picture in all of Scripture than Adam and Eve standing in the edge of that garden and knowing that they could no longer occupy it—that paradise that they'd known for a little while. And now they're driven out of it, leaving behind somewhere in that garden one of their boys dead on the ground. He was dead at the hands of the brother who now had preceded his father and mother out into the wilderness somewhere, condemned to wander and to try to make a life of his own. That's how it started as Genesis records it. It's as pitiful and pathetic a picture as you can imagine, isn't it—the consequence of the power of evil in the world?

God didn't explain why it was here. Jesus didn't explain why it was here. They both simply acknowledged that it **is** here. It has been here. Jesus didn't philosophize about it. He didn't try to take his disciples down in a session and go over in any kind of detail with them how it happened to be that the power of evil was present in the world. He just said, "It's here! And you've got to deal with it; or else it will deal with you."

I don't know how it started, perhaps innocently enough. She ran the store and had three children by him. He worked at another higher paying job that kept him away from the store during his working hours. A regular customer became too regular and her husband got off early one day and caught them at it. He ran to his truck, got his gun and she and her lover were both dead before he turned the gun on himself and ended it all. But it didn't end it all. Those three children had to be raised by their grandparents who were both in failing health, and what a legacy to have to overcome in life.

Temptation—you've got to deal with it, or if you don't deal with it, it will deal with you, and leave behind in its tragic wake such broken hearts and such shattered lives and such despair.

Jesus didn't go into any long dissertation about the problem of evil and temptation. He just said it's here, and you'd better do everything in your power to stay away from it. And that's why he put it into the prayer that we all know by heart and that we can say so easily—"Lead us not into temptation." Give me,

God, the power to use the intelligence that you have put into me, to stay away from the thing that I know can destroy me. I think that's what the prayer means, "Lead us not into temptation."

I took two of my granddaughters to the Circus in Albany back when Clyde Beatty was performing. I got so carried away up in the stands that I imagined myself in that role. I said to myself, "Wouldn't it be wonderful to be in that cage with those lions and tigers doing all those amazing things?" And in my mind I left my seat and walked down to the cage and as Clyde Beatty was coming out I said, "Mr. Beatty, I think I could do that."

"Oh," he says, "I'm not sure."

"Oh I think I can. Think of the applause I'd get if I did it, you know."

And so he said, "Well, if you want to try it, step inside."

So I stepped inside, and as I did, one of those lions said to one of those tigers, "That smells like preacher to me."

And those two animals began coming toward me and I ran frantically to the door and screamed, "God help me. What was in my mind?"

And God said to me, "Boy, you're praying five minutes too late. Five minutes ago before you left that seat, you should have prayed, 'God give me the capacity to sit in this seat and stay away from those animals in the cage.'"

You want to call me a coward because I won't go down and get inside the cage. OK, call me a coward. I'm still here, thank God.

Give me the power to use the intelligence that you have given me, Dear God, to know that there are things in this world that are more powerful than I and that can destroy me. And give me the power to stay away from them.

What does this have to do with folks like us—an established church, faithful for the most part? Why you couldn't sweep us out of heaven with a brush-broom anyway, could you? Aren't we just talking about drugs, or alcohol, or all kinds of things—sins of the flesh as we might call them? But there are sins of the spirit, and they come to attack us all.

Here's a minister, and I may or may not be just using my imagination. He allows himself to begin to think of the kind of appointment that he ought to have. And he looks at several who graduated from Emory at the same time he did, and he says, "Look at the appointments they have. And here I am still at this little place. The cabinet has forgotten me. The Bishop hasn't honored me. They haven't recognized my capacities and my abilities." And he begins to allow himself to feel jealousy and envy and he begins to be covetous of the positions and the places and the churches that are served by his contemporaries. And it isn't long before he begins to resent some of the men and women who occupy these places. And it isn't long before bitterness takes over his heart. And it isn't long before he begins to doubt whether or not he should be a minister. And the power of evil has possessed his spirit.

O God, keep me away from jealousy, keep me away from envy! Keep me away from looking around at what somebody else has and becoming resentful and bitter because I don't have it. Because it can only parch and shrivel my spirit until there is no life in it, and leave me a bitter thing that has no joy in life and offers no joy to anybody who lives around me. Oh, the power of evil is tremendous. It is significantly tremendous and it can destroy us. Jesus said, "Stay away from it."

Our youth used to say that somebody was chicken if they wouldn't do something risky or dangerous, meaning cowardly. I resent that. As a Methodist preacher I've always resented that. Because as a Methodist Preacher I respect chicken greatly. And I honor chicken greatly. And I do not like chicken associated with the word cowardly. I don't know who started that, and I don't like it. Oh you're chicken. You haven't got guts enough to face something. That's true. That's true. I've got intelligence enough to stay away from some of it, thank God. Because I know, I know what it can do to the human heart. I know what it can do to the human mind. I know what it can do to a life. I've seen the wrecks, shattered, all because they thought that they could handle what evil had to offer.

So take away from it its pleasures and its nice happy proprieties and see through to the dregs of it. That power of evil, the devil if you want to call it, Satan if you want to call it, whatever you want to call it, it's there! He will never be content until he has us drinking the dregs of it.

So that's the thing that Jesus said about it. Stay away from it. It's powerful. I'm not offering any explanation as to why it's here. I'm just telling you it's here. And I'm telling you, you better deal with it or else it will deal with you. That's what he said about it.

What he did about it, you know very well. He went into the wilderness. And according to this book, he stayed 40 days and 40 nights. And he fasted in that wilderness. And he went into the wilderness to face the power of evil. That's why he went there. That's what the book says. He went into the wilderness to struggle with the power of evil. Before he got active in his ministry, before he ever called a single disciple to follow him. After having been baptized by John and hearing God say, "This is my beloved Son," he went into the wilderness to struggle with the power of evil and to say there are some things I'm going to get settled before I ever start.

There's a wrestling match that I've got to be victorious in before I ever begin my ministry, and so he went into the wilderness to confront the power of evil. There where there was no temptation, where there was no ridicule, where there was no animosity, where there was no pressing crowd, there in the quiet of a wilderness place, he looked in his own life and he looked at the life of the world. And he acknowledged that the power of evil is a part of that world.

And he said, "I'm going to fight it right here and now. Every temptation that I think is likely to come to me, I'm going to look at it right now. Everything that the power of evil has to offer me as temptation, I'm going to examine it here and now. And I'm going to make my decision with reference to it. I'm going to decide. Here and now in the quiet of this place, where there is no struggle, where there is no pressure, where there is no hatred, I'm going to look at it. I'm going to examine it and I'm going to have the victory over it right here. So that when I get out there in the midst of it all and the pressures and the tensions and the temptations come, I'll say, I've already decided that. I already have my answer to that. I already know what I'm going to say. I had the victory over that months ago."

In the quiet of the wilderness place, because if you wait... The boy stumbled into my study and started crying. Something must have happened if the high school son of a prominent family in the church bursts into tears before his pastor. He'd been expelled from school an hour before, caught with an advance copy of the French final exam in his pocket while taking the test. He'd bought it from a guy for seventy-five cents in the restroom at school. He said, "Preacher, if it had ever occurred to me that anybody would ever offer me the answers to the final exam for seventy-five cents, I would have known that that was the cheapest, stupidest thing that I could ever do. But there he was in the restroom. I hadn't studied and the test was before me and I had the seventy-five cents in my pocket." Sometimes we don't have time to think.

Jesus said try to have time to think. Find you a wilderness place. Find you somewhere where you can look at your own life and you can look at the life of the world and think of the power of evil. Think how that power of evil can confront you, and what that power of evil can offer you in exchange for you. And decide right then and there in that quiet place, I would never do that. So help me God, I would never do that. There in your quiet place, having come to such a firm conviction, if then out there in the world where it all happens, if it comes, this power of evil, and puts the opportunity or puts the thought into your mind, you'll say, "O no, I decided that long ago. I know what my answer is. My answer is, No. My answer is, No."

When I reported for duty as a Navy Chaplain in Norfolk, I arrived there about a month before I had to go on a ship. I was sorry there was a war and sorry that I had to go and leave my family as a part of the war, but there was a kind of excitement about being in Norfolk. It was different from Camilla where I grew up where Rock Lake was just about the biggest body of water they had. I'd never seen anything in the lake or on the Flint River that was much bigger than a canoe or a little boat that people fish from. But there in Norfolk I saw the ships of the Navy. It was exciting for this landlubber to see those big ships of the Navy coming in to port at Norfolk. Each afternoon there were about two hours of free time and that's where I went every afternoon, down where the ships came in, down where the ships were tied.

One afternoon when I went down, there was the biggest thing I'd ever seen on land or sea tied alongside. It was bigger than the Hand Trading Company in Pelham was, and that was about the biggest thing I'd seen in my life. They could have put two or three football fields on the flight deck of that ship. I wondered how it could ever stay afloat. You'd think the bigness of it; the heaviness of it would just sink it. There it was. It was there for two weeks. Every afternoon I went by and I saw them carrying on board, lifting over into the hold of that ship every conceivable kind of supply. All kinds of food, all kinds of medical supplies, all kinds of mechanical things could be read from the labels on the boxes. They were being poured into that ship until it was full. One afternoon they were lifting planes over on to that deck. And one afternoon when I went down it was gone.

Some months later out in Idaho, in the Bachelor's Officer's Quarters at 11:00 o'clock, Whitey and I were listening to the late news. We were on our bunkers. We were listening to what a commentator was saying about a certain battle out in the Pacific. And he called the name of the ship. And he said that in the battle the ship was scarred, the ship was wounded, the ship was hurt, but it came out victorious in the battle. Whitey cut off the radio and I said, "Whitey, do you know where that ship won its battle?"

"Oh well," he said, "I guess out there in the Pacific, that's where it fought it."

No. I saw that ship winning its battle. It won its battle tied alongside the dock at Norfolk. There wasn't an enemy plane in sight, there were no submarines sighted out in the bay, there were no snipers in trees around the port of Norfolk. There wasn't any kind of hazard or danger to the ship as it was tied alongside. But there in the serenity and peace of it all, that ship was strengthening itself, and strengthening itself, and strengthening itself against the battle out there that awaited it on the sea.

We win our battles against evil when we pray, "O God, here's something I want you to help me with in advance." O God, O God, here's something I want you to help me with. It may come or it may not come, but if it comes I want to be prepared. I want my spirit to know its answer. I want my heart to have the word ready. I want my life to stand tall and straight in the presence of the power of evil, to say, "Get thee behind me, Satan!"

So we see Jesus there in the wilderness place. The devil said to him, "Hey, you're hungry aren't you?"

"Yes, come to think of it," said Jesus, "I am hungry. I've been here I don't know how long, but that little picnic lunch I brought along is long since gone. Yes, now that you remind me, I'm hungry."

"Well, if you're hungry," says the power of evil, "and if you're the Son of God as you claim to be, you have miraculous power. There are a bunch of stones lying here on the ground. Just take a few of them and hold them in your hand and say, 'Stones, be bread!' What's wrong with that? And eat the bread and have your hunger satisfied."

That sounds easy enough. That's sounds simple enough. That sounds like an interesting proposition.

"Ah," said Jesus. "It's not that simple. It isn't that simple, Mr. Devil. Anything you offer is never simple. It is not that simple. What you are asking me to do right here is what you will continue to ask me to do for my entire life here and that is to take some of the miraculous power that God has invested in me and use it for me! And under God I will not do that. I will never do that."

I'm no wagering man and I've nothing to bet, but I would wager with you that you could read this Gospel through a thousand times and never find one place where Jesus used his miraculous power to make anything easier for himself.

He was stretched out on that cross, and you will remember those raucous voices that came from below, "If you are the Son of God, come down! Use your power, if you are the Son of God. Work a miracle for yourself and step down from the cross, then we will believe you."

And if there was any moment of any sort of levity or amusement, if there was any moment of a kind of chuckling to himself that Jesus had on the cross, it was that moment. "Oh, I decided that long ago. I decided that long ago. I will never use my power to save me. I decided that in the wilderness place. I decided that in the quiet of the wilderness. In the presence of God, my Father, I made that decision and it's no temptation now."

So we follow the example of the Christ. Let's follow the example of the Christ here. If the veritable Son of God who was perfect in every way had enough respect for the power of evil to spend forty days in the wilderness struggling with it so that when he met it out in the thick of his life it would no longer be opposition to him, what do you think you and I ought to do? Do we have a quiet place? Are we going to use the forty days of the season of Lent to prepare to face the evil in our lives? If Jesus himself needed it, don't you think we just might?

Are we ready to close this service with this part of the prayer he gave us? I can make an altar here. You can make an altar where you sit. Are you ready for us to pray?

PRAYER

Father, lead us not into temptation, but deliver us from evil. For thine is the Kingdom and the power and the glory, forever. Amen

REGENERATION
(Nicodemus—The Night Visitor)
John 3:1-10, 7:45-52, 19:38-42 KJV

Have you ever found yourself doing something that you really had to do but later saying to yourself or someone else, "I did it, but my heart was not in it?" Or even more seriously, in the same sort of situation, "I found myself just going through the motions." There's no great spirit in it, there's no great joy in it any longer, and I'm just going through the motions. This is one of life's tragedies for us when we experience it, and from time to time, across the years all of us have to deal with this at some point or in some area of our lives. Where joy is gone, we miss it. But we're still confronted with the duties and responsibilities that have our names on them.

This was true of the man named Nicodemus. This had precisely happened to him. He was in the temple. He was a professional in the temple. He was a Pharisee. He was a righteous man. He knew the law from the beginning to the end. He knew all the rabbis' interpretations of the law. He obeyed the law. He interpreted the law to others. He went through all the rituals in the temple. He did his part. He celebrated from time to time in the varied festivals at the temple. He was a good man and he was a righteous man. But he came to Jesus, and what he seemed to be saying to Jesus by coming to him was, "I'm just going through the motions. I'm just going through the motions. But I have observed you. Sometimes I was sent to observe you."

And this was just stock in trade for the Pharisees after they began to discover the popularity of our Lord. And the kinds of amazing, miraculous things he was doing, and the things that he was saying that were so different, it seemed to them, from the law and their interpretation of the law. I think they started sending little delegations out all over Judea and Gallilee, wherever he was when they knew he was there. Three or four to stand on the edge, not to be too noticeable, but to listen intently to everything he said. Maybe to jot down some of the things that he said so that they could use those things against him later. Maybe to bring an end to all this confusion, this fuss, this carrying on about him that was prevalent wherever he was. And no doubt Nicodemus had been on such missions.

You recall that last week of his life when he was in Jerusalem every day—it was just over and over and over again. I don't really know how our Lord stood it. I don't know how he had the patience to do it. Sometimes I have thought that maybe it was a relief for him to finally be on the cross—rather than facing these ugly voices all day long—trying to trap him, trying to ensnare him, asking him questions every time he said anything, doing their best to find condemnation for him. No doubt Nicodemus was among those groups that were assigned that responsibility. "You go listen to him.

You go ask him questions. You go bring back a report."

And he was there that night when they brought him up before all these that were related to the temple. He tried to say something that was—positive. He couldn't say a lot. He knew all the evidence was against this man. He knew they were so prejudiced against him already that there was no way in the world that they could let him go free. He said the little he could say. He said, *"Our law doesn't judge people without first giving them a hearing to find out what they are doing, does it?"* (John 7:51)

But on this particular night he had to talk to him. He had to talk to him. Many have called Nicodemus a coward because he didn't go to Jesus in the daytime when it could be known that he was going to him, when some of his Pharisee brothers would see him there talking with him, apparently not condemning him or accusing him but searchingly talking to him about his own life. So he went at night. I don't condemn him for going at night. I praise him for going at all. Because it took a lot of courage. I've told people in my pastorates who have come to sit across from me in my study, "I know it wasn't easy for you to come here and I appreciate that." To go into the presence of any person to ask for help, to ask for advice, is never an easy thing. So he came to him at night and I'm thankful that he did.

He said, "I'm just going through the motions. I know how to do it all. I've done it all. It's all just habitual. I don't have to think about it. I just go through it. I say and do my part, but there's no joy, there's no feeling in it, there's no spirit in it. But I have heard you, and that's why I'm here. There seems to be spontaneity about your life. There seems to be joy in what you're doing. There's an infinite patience that I observe in you. And I've watched you in numbers of places, and I've been amazed at you. And I want to know how. I want to know how I could have it. Because I desperately need it. I desperately need it. I can't continue this way. I just can't continue this way. What can I do?"

And it's a pitiful cry. And unfortunately it's a familiar cry. I've had it made in my presence. "Pastor, we're just going through the motions in our marriage. That's all. All the heart's gone out of it, all of the spirit is gone, all of the joy is gone. And yet we are there together, and we'll be there together, because we are determined that we'll stay together, but there's no joy—all vanished someway. And we're caught now." It's a problem as familiar as this morning. "Jesus tell me, tell me, tell me what my need is."

"Well, Nicodemus, it's very clear. How was it when you began? How was it when you were born into all this? How was it with you when you presided in one of the festival worship services in the temple? How was it with you the first time you sat down with a young seeker and shared with him your knowledge of the Mosaic Law? And your understanding of the message of Isaiah, how was it as you shared it the first time?"

"O Lord, it was great. It was so great. I was exhilarated. I was so thankful to God that I was where I was. I was so humbled and yet so excited that I was in such a place. Every day was joy." "Well, Nicodemus, you were born into that. And you still experienced tragedies, the everyday occurrences where things go awry, but for the most part it was joy. You need to be born again, Nicodemus. You need to be born from above. You need to pray to God your father for this same spirit to pervade in your heart and life that you once knew. And that you thanked him for daily. You need to be born anew.

A new wind needs to blow across that dry, dry area of your life that you've allowed to be there. Let the wind blow. We don't know where it comes from, we don't know where it goes, but we feel it blowing gently across our bodies. And it's comforting, and it's soothing, and it's revitalizing. And if we walk feeling the wind, we walk under the spirit here, and if we're running we run with a little more vigor when we feel the wind flowing across our bodies—so with the spirit. Let the Spirit blow across those dry bones that your spirit has become. Ask, pray, acknowledge it as it begins to come as your father God helps you, enables you back to your first love. You can discover—rediscover all the joy that was there."

You remember how John had Christ speaking to that church at the beginning of the Book of Revelation, "You have left your first love. You've left all the joy of it. You've left the excitement of it. You've left the power of it. You've settled down to a dull routine just going through the motions of doing it without any joy. Your Father knows. Your Father will preside at your rebirth. And you will know it."

"This is not a secret, Nicodemus," Jesus said. "It's not a secret, but I'll share it with you. It is because my Father and I are one that you are able to observe in me a patience as I deal with hundreds and hundreds of people who clamor to hear my voice and feel the touch of my hand on their needy places. It's because of my intimacy with the Father that I'm able to move about in spite of all the things that you know about of which you have been a part. With a strong conviction still inside me that I'm doing what I'm doing and can know that it is his will for me to do it with joy. Not as if it was a punishment, not as if it had become a habit that I just go through the motions of doing, but because I'm dealing with his children, because I'm dealing with those who belong to him. And he loves them all."

"It is only through our Father God whom I share with in presiding at the new birth for you. You must be born again. There's no other way for it to come. You can't purchase it anywhere. You can't inherit it from anywhere. You can't borrow it from any of your associates among whom you live and with whom you work. It can come only from him."

Isn't it sad that when so many people find themselves in this situation of just going through the motions that they turn to all kinds of other things to try to revive their spirit? Sometimes a new affair—God, help us! Sometimes a new affair. You know what I mean. Sometimes a little more alcohol or more drugs either purchased on the street or more often prescribed in the office. Sometimes running up and down the seashores trying to find somewhere to plug in and find a little power. And it's not to be found anywhere. Only he, only he can give us the new birth. "You must be born again, Nicodemus."

Is our name Nicodemus? Does the shoe fit? Does the mood match where we've been, or maybe where we are? Have other solutions with us always come up short? Oh, I know we get weary. I know it's natural for us to just drag through certain days. I know that sometimes it seems like well, I just can't do it another day. But we dare not, O God, allow that pattern to repeat itself until it overwhelms our lives, until there's no spirit at all. Pray, pray daily—"O God, I need you to preside today. I need something new for this morning to send me through this day with joy. And I don't want to go through it any other way."

So John tells us that when Jesus died there on the cross, Nicodemus came. Isn't John a master storyteller? In his last words with Nicodemus in the night visitor incident, Jesus seems to be upbraiding him for not understanding the concept of being born from above. You don't know from that night visitor incident whether Jesus' words ever took with Nicodemus. But now we know. Nicodemus couldn't save him from the cross—I know that. Nicodemus knew that. You know that. He couldn't step out in the meeting of that group that night and say, "I demand that we free this man!" He knew that was hopeless. He was helpless to do anything about that. What can he do? And so John says he came. This dignified Pharisee, this man from the temple, this great professional of the religious life, appeared on Golgotha not in the night, but in the light with two sacks across his shoulders containing the precious spices. Anybody could see him now. Even the Pharisees could see him now. So with Joseph of Arimathaea he wound the white linen cloth around the body.

Some scholars tell us that he and the rich man, Joseph, must have used slaves to actually handle the dead body because if they had handled the body themselves they would have been ritually impure for seven days and therefore be unable to celebrate the

Passover feast. This would have been horrible for a pious Jew.

But I think there was a more powerful force at work here. Nicodemus with his hands inserted at every fold a handful of spices for his body. And I think with every handful that he placed, "Thank you, Lord. Thank you! Thank you!" Gratitude was the more powerful force. For a new spirit, a new joy came as a result of that blessed wind which is the Spirit blowing across the dryness of his heart and giving him new birth and new life.

And He'll do the same for you and for me. That's why I think John told this story. It's the gospel. It's the good news. I think he was saying, "It can happen to you just like that." You don't have to just keep going through the motions. You can be born from above. You can be born again. The wind of the Spirit can make your old dry bones live and you can have life and have it more abundantly. So go for it, pray for it daily. Let's pray for it right now.

Our heavenly Father,

- thank you for the blessed privilege of just sitting in this place
- and singing the familiar words to a blessed tune
- and looking around us and seeing the ones who are seeking that same faith
- and touching hand and heart and hugs with those we love who are about us.

- Thank you for this message that John has saved for us and for this good man who found an answer to his prayers. Help us to find answers to ours.
- And now, our heavenly Father, hold these your children close to your great heart of love.
- Remember with them today all those whom they love and for whom they greatly care.
- And travel with us through thy Holy Spirit for all the journeys that we make, through Christ our Lord. Amen.

RESURRECTION
(When He Calls Out Your Name)
Mark 16:1-2, 9, John 20:11-18 KJV

On this Easter morning I want to ask you, have you ever stood in your garden of loneliness, and fear, and depression, and difficulty, and failure and let your heart listen for a moment to hear the voice of the spirit of God speaking to you, calling your name so that you knew that you were not alone?

She was born in Magdala. That's one of the little villages along the Sea of Galilee. She was named Mary. The women were there inside the little house where the family lived. Eventually there was the cry of a baby, the newborn. And one of the women came to the door and said to the father and husband, who was sitting there, "It's a little girl."

He threw down the scone of bread he was munching on, "Why couldn't it have been a boy? A man's known for the sons he has, not his daughters!"

"What shall we name her? Your wife desires to know. What shall we call her?"

"Anything, Ruth, Naomi, anything you want to call her. Mary, whatever." And so she was Mary.

I imagine that she never really knew the love of a father. He never took her in his arms and comforted her when she was crying—never took her little fingers and walked along the sea and let her wade in the water. I feel she never knew that. And when she became old enough or at least thought she was, (and they never are), she decided that there must be something better than the life that she was living. So she left home as so many still do—hoping, daring to believe that something out there is better than what they know. And then finding that all that they can do is wander along the streets and then furtively, because there's nothing better open to the underage, unprepared woman, she offers her body for sale.

She was no longer a woman. She was no longer a person. She was possessed. There was only depression. There was only fear of the future. There was only shame for the present. There was only the realization that nobody really loved her. These men only lusted after her. They didn't care for her. They left their little money on the table for her and left and they were gone forever out of her life. But he came. He came.

I don't know where they met. I don't know how long they were together on that first visit. But something began to happen to Mary. They said demons had possessed her. And when you know one of them—fear, depression, guilt—it's a demon inside you choking the life out of you. There were several of them, they said. They were no match for him. And one by one he began to remove them from her hungry, lonely heart. She became a woman again. She became a person again. "Mary, I have a better life for you than the one you've found. And while many, many days and nights, particularly nights you felt that nobody loved you, He was loving you all the time, waiting for you to accept his love."

"He loves you. I love you. And there's a better life for you. There are people who are longing to be loved, and you have a capacity to love. Go find them, Mary. Go find them. Gift them with your life. Gift them with your love. Bring them within this circle to share with you the deliverance that you've experienced in your life and they'll be grateful forever."

And so he came to die. The little group of women that loved him, those that were related to him in their special ways were talking among themselves and they thought perhaps it would be best if they did not go. It was such a terrible thing to witness. All of the voices would be raucous, there'd be all kinds of obscenities, and it would be ugly and it would be horrible to watch. But Mary Magdalene said, "I'm accustomed to all of that. They can't shock me. There isn't really much that I haven't experienced or seen, and I'm going. I'm going." She told Mary the Mother, "I know you want to go. And I will go."

"Thank you, Lord, for saving my soul"…we sing a little chorus. "Thank you, Lord, for saving my soul." I'm sure Mary Magdalene from that day forward became one of his finest witnesses—went out to tell the story of his love. She may very well have been the first to understand that this cross was a symbol of the love of God, that it was not an ugly, shameful thing. It was the means by which God would say to the world, "I love you and this is the extreme to which I'll go to give my only begotten Son to show my love and to bring to you the forgiveness that your heart needs so sorely."

And so she went there to the foot of that cross. "I know I'm not very much. I know, God, I'm not very much. I know that you can't claim very much because of what you did for me. But I want you to know that here I am—one grateful that you came and touched my life and delivered it. And I had to come here to say, 'Thank You.' I don't want you to die without knowing how grateful I am for what you did for me. And I know there are others besides me. You may feel that you have failed because you are hanging there suffering in all that shame. But there are many like me that would like to kneel here and thank you for the salvation you brought, who'll be forever grateful as I am."

Mary, on that morning before anyone in the house had awakened, seemed to have been awake all night long, waiting for the coming of the dawn. She finally couldn't wait until the dawn broke, but began her walk to the tomb where they had laid him. In her hand was an alabaster box and it was filled with precious spices. "If by chance, God, someone would roll that stone away for me that I might touch him one more time, and kneel there in the presence of his lifeless body and thank him again for what he's done for me."

But there was no stone. There was no body. "Where have you taken him? Where is he?"

And she ran back to the house to say, "He's not there. I've been, and he's not there."

And several of the disciples ran there to see and they ran back again. But Mary remained. She walked out into the little garden that marked the place where the tomb was. And standing there desolate she sees a figure. And she assumes that it's the gardener who has come early to do his chores and wants to be there at the first break of the sun so that he can begin to do it in the cool of the day. And she speaks to the gardener, "Have you taken him away? Have you taken him away? If you have taken him away, tell me where you have taken him. And I will be strong to take his body, and take him to those who love him."

And he turned and he spoke to her—"Mary". And she knew. It was her Lord.

If I had been planning the resurrection I wouldn't have done it that way at all. And that's why God didn't let me do it. I would have wanted a crowd there. I would have wanted all of them there. I would have wanted the priests and the scribes and the rabbis. I would have wanted the Roman Soldiers, particularly those that drove the nails into his hands. I would have wanted Pilate and Herod sitting front center. And I would have wanted all the people of Jerusalem who could crowd into that area. And when all were present and the sun was beginning to break on the horizon, I would let the stone roll away and let him emerge from the tomb. And I'd let him stand there in all his resplendent glory, to reveal to them and to the world that he was the risen Lord. But he didn't do it that way.

One woman! One woman! And she hadn't been a very good woman all her life. That's for sure. And she hadn't always been pleasing even to herself by any means. That's for sure. And she hadn't been loved much in her life until he came along. That **was** for sure. And it was to that one woman that he first revealed himself when he came forth from the tomb. And he called her name, "Mary."

And she came to life and she knew that it was her Lord. And suddenly he was there no longer, and she ran back to the house and said, "I saw the Lord! He is alive!" And I think she added—not as a postscript, but as the chief emphasis in her pronouncement,

"He called me by my name. He called me by my name."

You've been standing in a garden like that. And if you haven't, one day you will, one day you will—garden of disappointment, garden of loneliness, a garden of fear, a garden of guilt, a garden of ultimate depression. You'll be standing there. And you'll be wondering, "Is there anybody, is there anybody who really cares?" And if you let your heart listen, and if everything is quiet as your heart listens, you may hear him call **your** name—"Mary, Sarah, Ruth, George, Jim". And you will know that you are not alone. You will know that he loves you. You will know that he cares for you. You will know that he is everlastingly with you. You, too, will leave your garden, and you will make your pronouncement, "He is alive! And he called me by my name."

O eternal God and our heavenly father, give us vigorous faith to believe with all of our hearts that nothing can happen to us, no experience can come to us, no emotion overwhelm us without the awareness of it in your great heart of love. Grant us to believe in this Jesus Christ who walked this earth revealing to us this great and wondrous faith that you care for each of us. Now hold all these dear children close to your great heart of love along with all of those whom they love and for whom they greatly care. And grant us your spirit's presence on the journeys that we make including the last one. We make our prayer in the name of the one who calls out our name, even Jesus Christ, our risen Lord. Amen.

Frederick Wilson with "Cile" Crouch and Evelyn Dann, installing the new President of the Woman's Society of Christian Service at First Methodist Church, Albany, Georgia circa 1960.

EVANGELISM
(Does Anybody Care?)
Luke 15:1-24

One of the games that we used to play growing up, we called Hide and Go Seek. I don't know if it's played anymore. Children don't seem to play games as we used to play them. That was one of our favorite games to play out at night, which we were quite at liberty to do in our little town, and we played Hide and Go Seek very often. We would go "Eeny, Meeny, Miney, Mo" until we identified who would be "It". Then "It" would get up against the tree and count 500 by fives and everybody would go hide, and then "It" would go find whoever had hid, and having sighted them would run back to the tree and hopefully outrun the one that had been found. 'Twas a nice game, perfectly innocent and sometimes exciting. One afternoon I remember there was a group at our house and we all said, "Let's play Hide and Go Seek."

There was a little girl who had come from down the street and she said she didn't want to play "Hide and Go Seek." Well, there is always one like that who doesn't want to play what everybody else wants to play, but she was very insistent. She said, "I don't like to play Hide and Go Seek".

"Well, why don't you like to play Hide and Go Seek?

She said, "I'm scared I'll get hid and nobody will come to find me."

And that's what thousands of people are afraid of across the world. They are desperately afraid that somebody will not come to find them when they are hid away in some lonely anguish of spirit. Sometimes it's anguish that they have brought upon themselves. This is the haunting fear that possesses the heart. I will be hid and no one will come to find me.

Jesus told three stories about things and persons that were lost. They are recorded in that wonderful 15th chapter of The Gospel According to Saint Luke. I thought many a time, if I had to surrender all else from the Bible, and could keep only one chapter, I believe I would keep the 15th chapter of The Gospel according to Saint Luke, because this is the gospel, and this is evangelism.

"Little coin, how did you get lost?"
"Well, I didn't have anything to do with getting lost. My mistress had me in her hand and she was looking at me, and admiring me and she was so proud of me. I was a new addition to her headpiece. There were nine other pieces and now I was the tenth, and that completed that lovely, lovely thing that rested on her forehead. She was so proud of me, and in her excitement, as she admired me, she dropped me from her hand. And I was round, and I started rolling. I rolled and rolled over the hard floor, and then came to rest in a very obscure part of the room.

I didn't have anything to do with getting lost. I didn't want to get lost, I didn't intend to get lost, I didn't try to get lost, I didn't do anything to help me to get lost. My mistress just dropped me from her hand. But, oh, I was so lost! I was so alone! I was in the dark, in a part of the room where no one would ever see me. It didn't matter that I didn't have anything to do with my getting lost. I was lost, I was very lost."

"Little lamb, how did you get lost?"

"Oh, I got lost because I was careless. I got lost because I was a little reckless. I got lost because I forgot what my shepherd told me. I didn't intend to get lost that day either. I didn't start out that morning with the other sheep saying to myself, I'm going to get lost today. I'm going to get *lost* today! I didn't start out like that. I started out just like all the other sheep started out, to feed on the pastures to which our shepherd would lead us. Our shepherd brought us to the green pastures and he told us to graze on the tender green grass that he had found for us on the hillside. And I started doing precisely that. My little head was down. Oh, the grass was so succulent, so tasty, and so wonderful after the dry months. I just kept nibbling away, walking as I nibbled, nibbling as I walked, 'til suddenly I turned around and I was alone, and I knew I was lost. There was no shepherd and there were no other sheep, and I was on the mountainside alone.

I hadn't planned it that way. I didn't start out that morning saying I'm going to wind up at eventide alone on the mountainside. I had no intention of that happening, but there I was. It was growing dark. Already I could hear the sounds of the mountains, and I knew that I was alone, and that I was helpless and that I was lost. And it hadn't mattered and it didn't matter that I didn't intend to get lost, that my carelessness and my recklessness was responsible for my being lost. I was still lost, a little lamb without a shepherd."

"Boy, how did you get lost?"

"Oh, sir, I'm sorry you asked that question. It's a very embarrassing question to have to answer. I got lost because I willfully left my home. I knew, at least I thought I knew what I was doing that morning when I asked my father to play dead and give me my part of the inheritance. I was sick of that place. I was tired of home. I was worn out with my mother and father. I was plain disgusted with my family, and with the dullness of my life. I talked to several of the caravan as they came by and tented on our ground, and they told me about a land out there that I didn't know anything about, that I had never experienced, never tasted. It all sounded so exciting in contrast to the dull, boring life that I was living in this house and on this place where I was living with my parents, and with my brother and my sisters.

So, I made up my mind I would ask my father for what belongs to me to come to me. So, I asked him to play like he was dead. Give me my part of the inheritance without requiring me to wait on this dull place until he did die and I got what was coming to me. To my utter surprise he gave it to me. And I left home and I followed the direction of the caravan. As a matter of fact, I followed the caravan and they led me into that city. Oh, what a city! What excitement! What joys! What thrills! What new experiences!

Gradually my money began to dwindle and to my great and utter and terrifying surprise my friends dwindled with my money. And suddenly I was aware that there was a famine in the land. There were no jobs. There was no food. There was nothing. I had no friends, I had no job, I had no money. Someone told me there was a Gentile who lived on the edge of this city who raised hogs for the Romans who peopled the land. You will know the extent of my lost-ness when I tell you I went to that man's door and asked him if he would allow me, the son of a Jewish family, to feed the hogs. And he told me that I could go down to the pigsty and feed his hogs. And I sat down in that pen shelling corn for those pigs and I said to me, 'Boy you are lost. You are really lost!'"

"Little coin, did you stay lost?"
"No, I didn't stay lost. I didn't stay lost. You know the very second that my mistress felt me slip from her hand, she was down on her hands and knees looking for me. The room became dark as day began to dwindle and she found a candle, she found a little lamp, one in each hand as she started looking across the floor for me. One time she got so close and I wanted to cry out, 'You're getting hot, you're getting

hot!' But then she turned in another direction and I was still lying there lost. She blew out her candle and she walked out the door and I thought, Oh, I shall remain lost forever. She has gone away and she will never find me. I will be covered in the dust that accumulates in this part of the house and I will never be found.

Suddenly the room was filled with light. My mistress hadn't forgotten me at all. She had gone to her neighbors and she had said to her friends, I have lost a coin. Bring your lamps and help me find the coin that I have lost. The room was ablaze with light as all were down on their hands and knees, and my mistress came crawling across the floor and saw me and reached out her eager and searching fingers and held me close again. No, I didn't stay lost. There was someone who loved me and came looking for me until she found me."

"Little lamb, did you stay lost?"
"No, I didn't stay lost. I didn't stay lost. I wasn't lost much longer than midnight, no thanks to me but thanks to my shepherd. Dark had come on and I crouched down under a bush on that mountain, frightened to death and shaking with the cold. It was the first night I had ever spent outside the fold on a chilly night. I was shaking from fright and shaking from the cold, and the noises and the sounds in the mountains became like thunder roars, terrifying me. It seemed to me that I could hear all around me the feet of those animals about whom I had heard the

shepherd speak that were preying upon the lives of little innocent lambs who were helpless as he told us that we must stay close to the shepherd.

I thought that I shall never, ever see light again. And I shall never, ever see the face of my shepherd. And I will never, ever again join the flock, the herd, the sheep with whom I have run these days.

Suddenly there was a noise that seemed to be familiar. 'Padafoot!' That's my name. 'Padafoot! Padafoot!' A voice was calling my name all across that mountain. And I started bleating, knowing that it was my shepherd, assured that it was my shepherd, and not someone in wolves clothing coming to snatch my life away. And I bleated, and bleated and bleated with all of my voice. And suddenly there he was. There he was! He reached down and picked me up and held me close to him.

I thought, when he picks me up he's going to wring my neck. I thought, when he picks me up he's going to shear me right here on this mountain. Just think of all these miles that I've made him walk. He's come out here on this mountain all alone exposing himself to the threat of all these noises and the threat of getting lost in the dark.

But oh, when he found me he unloosed his garment and held me against his very skin to warm me. He kept running his hand up and down my wooly coat. 'Oh, Padafoot, I found you, I found you, I found you. The other shepherds said, "You're stupid to go out on that mountain. You've got ninety-nine sheep here. That's a mighty good average. You're doing mighty well to come home every night with ninety-nine. Don't, don't worry about the one. Probably gone by now anyway." But, oh, Padafoot, I couldn't sleep thinking about you out here somewhere. I'm so glad I found you.' He brought me home."

"Boy, did you stay lost?"

"No, I didn't stay lost. I began to discover who I was in that pigpen. The first thing I discovered in that pigpen was that I was not a pig. And I said to myself, 'Here I sit in a pigpen and I am not a pig.' I was not made to be a pig. I was not created to be a pig. I was not born to be a pig. My name is not pig. But here I sit in a pigpen. I'm not going to stay in this pigpen. I wasn't made to live in a pigpen. I wasn't made to live in the filth and the muck and mire of a pigpen. And the lowest servant in my father's house has on a clean robe this morning and here I sit in the mud of this pigpen. I'm not going to stay here. I wasn't meant to be here. So, I'm going home. I'm going home.

So, what will I say to my father, the father that I asked to play dead? Well, I'll make me up a speech. So, with my big toe, I wrote in the mud. *'Father I have sinned against heaven and in your sight and am no more worthy to be called your son.'* I thought, that's a good speech. I know I am not a pig, because a pig couldn't write a speech like that with his big toe. Pig couldn't even think of a speech like that. No, I'm not a pig. I'm a son. I'm a child. I'm a boy, and I belong. I didn't even go up to the house to tell the man I was leaving. I just climbed over that pig- sty and started home.

I kept saying my speech. *'Father, I have sinned against heaven and in your sight and am no more worthy to be called your son. Make me a hired servant in your house.'* I'd walk another mile and I'd say my speech. *'Father, I have sinned against heaven and in your sight and am no more worthy to be called your son. Make me a hired servant in your house.'* I'd walk another mile and I'd say my speech. I could say it backward. I could pick it up in the middle and say it in either direction. I knew my speech. I knew my speech right and left. I knew when I came into the presence of my father he would be impressed with my speech. *'Father, I have sinned against heaven and in your sight and am no more worthy to be called your son.'*

And there is the road and the last turn in that road is home. Oh, no! I can't do it. How does a boy go and say anything to a father that he has asked to play dead? Maybe I **am** a pig. What will he say? What will he say? What will he **do**, not what will he say. What will he **do**? I can't imagine what he will do. I know what I'd do if my boy asked me to play dead, give me what belonged to me so that I could go from this boring place. Oh, I can't go. I can't go. My eyes teary and coming down my cheeks. The sun setting, nearly blinding me with its brilliance. I look up the hill and there is a figure at the top of the hill. It's my father. Oh, what was the speech, what was the speech? How does the speech begin? What was the first word of the speech? How does the speech go? What was the speech trying to say? I can't think of the speech. I can think of nothing but being terrified. There's my father and he has the advantage of the hill. He can run down the hill if he sees me, if he eyes me, if he recognizes me. He can run down the hill and with the strength of his body crush me into these stones on which I am standing and then with his feet stomp me in the earth. What good is a speech? And suddenly the figure moved. The figure moved down the hill and 'twas too late to run—too late to do anything but try to think of the speech. I got the first word, *'Father.'* Yes. *'I have sinned.'* Yes. By that time my father was in reach. Here it comes. My father suddenly stopped. Those arms, instead of against me, and those fists instead of balled and on my head were arms and hands around me, clasping. And there was crying, sobs and a wet cheek put against mine, and then, to the other one in sweet embrace.

> *'Father, I have sinned against heaven.'*
> "Hush boy, you're home."
> *'Father, I have sinned against...'*
> "Hush boy, you're home!"

No, I didn't stay lost. There was somebody that loved me and when he sighted me coming home he ran to claim me as his own. No, I didn't stay lost."

Jesus Christ came into the world to say, "God is a seeking God and you will never ever be able to hide from your seeking God". It doesn't matter *why* you are lost, it doesn't matter *how* it happened that you are lost, it doesn't matter *the extent* to which you are lost. If you are lost, God will come to find you. Jesus said, "This is the kind of God you have as your Father, this is the kind of Savior that you have in me, the Christ. If you are lost you are not forgotten and someone will come looking for you. It will be the Christ. It will be your Father, God."

I didn't stay lost, said the little coin. Somebody loved me. I didn't stay lost, said the little lamb. Somebody loved me. I didn't stay lost, said the boy. Somebody loved me. Jesus said that somebody is God your Father, and that somebody is Christ, your Savior. And that is the Christ of evangelism.

There are a lot of lost people out there. That doesn't mean they are necessarily going to hell. They're just lost. They aren't found. They're lost because they aren't found. They are lonely people. They are defeated people. They are people who have lost any zest or enthusiasm about life. They are people who think everybody hates them. A lot of young people think everybody hates them. People have gotten on the wrong road and they are lost. There are just a lot of lost people out there. They need to know that somebody loves them. That's what they need to know—precisely what the little coin knew.

There are a lot of people who get lost through no fault of their own. They didn't intend to get lost, they didn't plan to get lost. They didn't design their lives as a lost life. In many cases it was somebody else's fault, something that somebody else did—pushing them, shoving them 'til they were lost. Dropping them carelessly, recklessly, but they're lost, just as lost as if they had done it themselves. They're out there wondering if anybody cares, wondering if anybody loves.

There are a lot of people out there that are lost that just got lost carelessly. They didn't know that when you pick up this end of the stick you also get the other end of the stick. They meant well. They didn't mean any harm. They didn't mean to hurt themselves. They didn't mean to get the habit. They just started and just kept nibbling away without looking back to see where they were going. Suddenly they had the habit. Suddenly they were too far from home to find the way back alone. They are out there wondering if anybody cares and if anybody loves them.

Some of them almost look as if they planned to get lost, meant to get lost. Some of them asked God to play dead and act as if He didn't exist at all so they could just go their way, doing their thing, having their will, living their lives without reference to anybody else or to any god anywhere.

There are a lot of people who have gotten lost that way. They intended it, willed it, saw to it. Now they are buried in their lostness, the pigpens of their lostness, and they are beginning to feel that they are not pigs. But they wonder if anybody else feels that they are not—if anybody cares, if anybody loves them.

And evangelism is simply going to say, "I care." Evangelism is going simply to say, "God loves you." Evangelism is simply going to say, "You have a Savior." You don't have to make big speeches. You don't have to make long talks. You don't have to get involved in a long discussion of God and His mercy and love. You just go and say I care, and God your Father through Jesus Christ loves you and wants you to come home—wants you to come home. You can be that kind of evangelist. You never know when God will give you the opportunity to be an evangelist. In the name of Christ, you can simply to say to some lost and lonely soul, I care and God loves you.

Prayer

O God, we lift our prayer for all the lost and lonely people. But even as we pray for them we know that we are really praying for ourselves. Grant that our hearts may be so caring that as we point out the way to others, we, too, may find our way home. In the name of the Shepherd and Savior of our souls, even Jesus Christ our Lord. Amen.

RECONCILIATION
(On Being Ministers of Reconciliation)
By W. Hamp Watson, Jr.
(With indebtedness to J. Frederick Wilson for the approach to the subject.)

"All this is from God, who through Christ reconciled us to himself and gave us the ministry of reconciliation; that is, in Christ, God was reconciling the world to himself, not counting their trespasses against them and entrusting to us the message of reconciliation." (II Corinthians 5:18-20 RSV)

The tragedy of our life and our time is the tragedy of broken relationships. The father in the family was dying of cancer. He and his sister had not spoken to each other in years. His daughter was distraught because time was running out for her aunt and her Daddy to seek forgiveness of each other, and neither would make a move. The tangled web of broken relationships was a barrier preventing his going home to God in peace and she felt helpless to do anything about it. The tragedy of our time is this tragedy of broken relationships.

Sitting in his living room, Tommy Pritchett told me something it would have been hard for me to believe unless I had heard it as I did from his own lips. Pinned in his M.G. after an accident, he could smell the fumes of the gas escaping from a burst tank.

He knew an explosion could be imminent. Through the glass he saw the white face of a truck driver that had seen the wreck and stopped. He cried, "Get me out of here!"

Taking no action to help at all the truck driver said, "Who are you? Are you white or black?"

Tommy could hardly believe what he heard but he quickly yelled through the blood on his face, "White, white!"

He was promptly hauled out to safety and he said that on the way to the hospital, the truck driver told him it was a good thing that he had said "white", for if he had said "black" he would have left him there. The tragedy of our life and our time is the tragedy of broken relationships.

You can see it in some communities where economic and social groupings are clearly delineated, and never the twain shall meet. I heard a newcomer to another community express it this way: "Blank is a miserable place. If you were born there, you belong to that crowd. If you're in the new paper mill, you're in that crowd. If you are neither, you're a fifth wheel, you're a nobody."

You can see it in churches where bitterness has come between people who once were friends. Two classes used to be together before some friction came up. They are asked if they'll merge. Their attendance now only justified one teacher. The spokesman for one class says to the superintendent, "I don't know whether we can do that or not. They sing three hymns and we sing only two."

A man was describing one of those bumper to bumper traffic jams on the freeway where they were repairing an exit ramp. He said, "There we were, driving temper to temper."

Drunkenness and marital infidelity rank high as the causes of broken relationships in marriage, but so often these are the last stages. Most trouble starts at a much seemingly milder level. They sit across the desk from the counselor. He says, "She never has my clothes ready right. I don't know when I go out but what I might have on a blue and black sock." What earthly difference should this make? How many of you this morning would notice whether I had on one black sock and one blue one? Would I get fired as your pastor? Imagine my going in at dinner and saying to Day, "Can't you ever do anything right? Are you color blind? Don't you know black from blue? What did I buy those glasses for you for? You think nothing of embarrassing me before the whole town, do you? Didn't your mother teach you anything about sorting socks?"

Does it sound silly and insignificant? Yet blows are exchanged and marriages break over a piling up of such seemingly silly incidents. Judge Taylor Phillips told about a wife who wanted a divorce on the basis that her husband was careless about his appearance. She said, "In fact, Judge, he hasn't shown up in two years." Vocation, finances, housekeeping, in-laws, child training, sex, social life, and drinking all come in for their count in the conflict. But what little things in a family lead to the tragedy of broken relationships!

Speaking to all these situations there comes a beautiful word from the Bible—Reconciliation. It can be defined as being right with our brothers and sisters, being right with our loved ones, being right with God. O be ye reconciled! The most beautiful word in the language! "In Christ, God was reconciling the world unto himself."

When relationships are broken we try to make ourselves believe that it doesn't really matter. "I don't care if she never speaks to me again." But the words sound hollow. We aren't really very successful at convincing ourselves. Something pulls at us and tears at the flesh of our spirits. There comes a word here, an old picture, a flash here, a face that smiled and we remember with pain, "That's the way it was. It used to be." God has made us this way.

The mother told me with tears how she sacrificed to send her daughter away to California to school. Out there she fell in love with a man who was a member of a radical religious sect. She said, "I told her if she joined his church she could count on no more support from me; and, if she married him, she need not ever come back home." But she said, "I get letters from her now, trying to convert me to her new found faith. She hasn't married him but she's joined with him. Her tuition is due and I have it saved for

her next quarter. Should I write her? Should I send
her the money? She's a good girl. I love her. I reared
her in my church. How could we be this far apart?"

I could tell she wanted to write her daughter.
Without saying it outright, her daughter's
last letter had "Take me back" ringing all through it.
We long for reconciliation. It is so with God.
Something down inside knows—"There is God and I
am His. I'm his child. Something of Him is stamped
on me. I try to write it off, but it matters." As
Augustine put it, "Thou hast made us for thyself, and
our hearts are restless until they rest in thee." This is
God's business—reconciliation.

But according to the Bible this is your
business, too. *"All this is from God, who through
Christ reconciled us to himself and gave us the
ministry of reconciliation." "In Christ God was
reconciling the world to himself"* but he was also
"entrusting to us the message of reconciliation."
Could that really be true? You and I entrusted with
something that beautiful? Are we sent to the broken
relationships of our day with the message of
reconciliation? If the tragedy of our life and our time
is the tragedy of broken relationships, can we share
the glorious news for our time that we can be
reconciled?

People are making me believe it. I rejoiced
some time back when a Christian couple from that
former church told me they were working with that

distraught daughter to help her deal with her dying Daddy's unrelenting hatred of his sister. I don't know how they're going to do it, but Paul says they're called to do it, entrusted with it—they're going to be ministers of reconciliation!

A minister of reconciliation can be a teacher like the one that told me she was going to do her best to help the minority child in her classroom. This was back before the massive integration in our Georgia schools in 1971. She said her determination came on the opening day of school when the little girl went to the back corner of the room and covered her face with her hands. With joy she told me how the children had accepted her and the progress she was making.

Halford Luccock told about a layman that was behind every worthy church and community effort in a large city. A committee was appointed in this great church to select a stained glass window that would memorialize this giant of the faith. They discussed the Christian symbol that ought to go at the center— the triangle for the Trinity, the ship for the Church, the dove for the descending Spirit of God.

But one woman spoke up and said, "I know, the symbol ought to be a glue-pot."
They said, "Why?'
She said, "Well, he literally held this church and community together. It ought to be a glue pot."

Every good pastor has experienced it. Here are two persons who have grown apart because of little things that have become big things. What a thrill and joy it is to see them sit down together and begin to hammer out some concrete changes that they can make in their marriage to preserve it and enrich it. They, themselves, become ministers of reconciliation, as they minister to each other with their first halting efforts toward self-understanding and real behavioral change.

The girl was nineteen and a half and had just given birth to her first child—a baby boy. Her pastor, Dr. Frederick Wilson, called on her in the hospital room. He was especially concerned for she had a rather brash, irresponsible young husband who was fast and loose with his commitments. While Frederick was in the room, the young husband came in.

"Have you seen my boy, Dr. Wilson?"

"No, I haven't, yet."

"Do you have any boys, Dr. Wilson?"

"No, we have some wonderful daughters."

"Oh, you never had a boy. Come on down here to this window and I'll show you what a real boy looks like."

Frederick quickly followed the husband out and down the hall. When they got to the window he said, "So you never had a boy. That's a boy baby. Take a look at him, preacher. I don't guess you know what it means to feel like a real father, do you? Take a look at a boy. That's a real boy!"

Frederick said, "Yes, God has given you a fine baby boy, I hope you'll be worthy of him." And he turned and walked away down the hall.

Frederick said, "I don't know when he started running after me, but I soon felt his hand on my shoulder and he pushed me toward a chair as he said, 'Forgive me, Preacher. Pray God to forgive me.'"

Frederick did just that and more. They went back into the room for a real visit and Frederick said, "Would you have thought that boy wanted to be reconciled?"

And so it is that none of us can hold our peace or be uninvolved in the presence of

- that love on a cross that broke down the dividing wall of hostility,
  - that love that passed by in Jesus of Nazareth,
    - and is still passing by in every miracle of reconciliation
      - and every act of redemptive love in our time.

This is God's business—reconciliation! O be ye reconciled! And once reconciled, become yourself a minister of reconciliation for, *"All this is from God, who through Christ reconciled us to himself and gave us the ministry of reconciliation."*

GIVEN TO GRACIOUS HUMOUR

Frederick said, "Early in our marriage, one of the chores that I took on for myself was to make up the bed every morning. This was not just to help Henry Kate, though I was glad to do that. It was so that I could say even before I had left home for the tasks that would be waiting, 'At least I've accomplished **one** thing today.'"

Albert Reichert remembers Frederick telling about the Custodian at St. Paul United Methodist Church in Columbus. His first name was Moses. Frederick said, "Moses was often alone at the church when the telephone rang. He took delight in answering, 'This is St. Paul's Church. Moses speaking.'"

In his retirement talk at Annual Conference, Frederick reflected on what it was like as he and Henry Kate began their ministry serving a country circuit of churches in Twiggs County, Georgia at the end of the depression. The little churches couldn't always come up with even the money to pay their pastor's salary, but they gave generously of what they had—eggs, country ham, sausage, sweet potatoes—as their substitute for preacher pay. They didn't have enough cash to buy any clothes.

Frederick said, "One day when I had come back to the parsonage with no money, but with the back seat of the car loaded with farm produce, Henry Kate said, 'Frederick, at this rate we're soon going to be the fattest naked people in this county.'"

Steve Rumford, President of The Methodist Home for Children and Youth, recalls the day the Home dedicated the Frederick Wilson Administration Building to him. It was the fall before he died. They had unveiled the portrait of Frederick and Henry Kate that now adorns the lobby of that building. A string of speakers got up one after the other extolling the virtues of this man who had been President of the Trustees for the Home and had chosen to spend his retirement years in a home on the campus. Frederick sat there somewhat embarrassed by it all. When he was finally allowed to get up to respond he said something like this:

"Some day not too far removed from now, a friend of yours is going to call you and ask you if you would join him and go to Old Brother Frederick Wilson's funeral. And your response will be, 'I think I've already been to that funeral.'"

INDELIBLE IMPRESSIONS

Sue Taylor wrote, "This was sent to my family and me after Mother died in February of 1977. You can imagine the comfort my family and I received from this 'handwritten' note."

Christmas, 1977

Dear Sue and family,
During the year I am aware that you have lost by death someone dear to you. I know that at Christmas, more than any other time, we miss those who have been a part of our lives to bless them.
I want you to know that you and your family are in my thoughts and prayers.
May joyous memories fill your heart and dispel its loneliness and may the Christ of Christmas be peace and comfort to you.
"...and with the morn those angel faces smile which I have loved long since and lost a while."
Most sincerely, with affection,
Frederick

At Dooly Campground where Frederick was preaching, he had been called back to a pastorate for a funeral. Several of us "young preachers" who were sitting under the Tabernacle saw his car pull on to the campus. With a note of wondering awe in his voice, Jim Jensen said, "The **Man** is back!"

Camilla Humber remembered, "The first Sunday Frederick preached at our Church he introduced himself saying, *'You can call me Brother or Frederick or Fred. Please don't call me Freddy.'* He was definitely not a 'Freddy'! He was an elegant man but with a jaunty, bouncy gait. He was probably the most spiritual person I have ever known and he had a great sense of humor. He made the Bible come alive in the pulpit and could read Roark Bradford's <u>All God's Children</u> to Family Night Supper with obvious delight. He played the piano and sang a ditty called "Miss Otis Regrets" at a Sunday school class party. Frederick was truly a 'Renaissance Man'!

Betty Mackey said, "I knew that God would have someone in place during the dreadful time of 'The Strangler'. What a wonderful and gracious God to have provided Frederick Wilson for our assurance and comfort."

Alice Fraser said, "When Frederick would walk down the aisle after the morning service, I felt the breeze from his robe and I always felt that a saint had just blessed me."

A

FEW

FADED

PHOTOGRAPHS

Frederick and Brad Brady relating to youth on the Campus of the Methodist Home for Children and Youth in Macon, Georgia

Best Wishes for Christmas
and the New Year

Chaplain Frederick Wilson, U.S. Navy, in World War II

Chaplain Wilson and Sailors on New Guinea in World War II

FREDERICK AND HENRY KATE GARDNER WILSON